"Quality tools in the hands of a skilled worker create things of beauty and value. *Acts 29* provides those tools that, in the hands of a person who embodies Christ, can be used to draw people to him. Churched people especially will find *Acts 29* a valuable resource as they follow Jesus into and among a world of hurting, broken, messy, and—in God's eyes—beautiful and valuable people."

—ERIC STOLTE, president, The Navigators of Canada

"*Acts 29* makes clear the content of the gospel, the context for its reception, and the confidence available to any willing Christian who, as a 'worker together with God,' will participate in his agenda of bringing people to himself. It is refreshing, relevant, and realistic and will open doors of opportunity to anyone with open eyes."

—CHARLES PRICE, senior pastor,
The Peoples Church, Toronto, Canada

ACTS 29

"You've had your chance. The non-Jewish outsiders are next on the list. And believe me, they're going to receive it with open arms!" Paul lived for two years in his rented house. He welcomed everyone who came to visit. He urgently presented all matters of the kingdom of God. He explained everything about Jesus Christ. His door was always open.

The Mission Continues . . .
A Course in Sharing Your Faith

CHRIS KOVAC

NAVPRESS⬤

NavPress is the publishing ministry of The Navigators, an international Christian organization and leader in personal spiritual development. NavPress is committed to helping people grow spiritually and enjoy lives of meaning and hope through personal and group resources that are biblically rooted, culturally relevant, and highly practical.

For a free catalog go to www.NavPress.com
or call 1.800.366.7788 in the United States or 1.800.839.4769 in Canada.

ISBN-13: 978-1-60006-312-1

Cover design by Hugh Syme, Hugh Syme Studios

Some of the anecdotal illustrations in this book are true to life and are included with the permission of the persons involved. All other illustrations are composites of real situations, and any resemblance to people living or dead is coincidental.

Unless otherwise identified, all Scripture quotations in this publication are taken from the *Holy Bible, New International Version*® (NIV®). Copyright © 1973, 1978, 1984 by International Bible Society. Used by permission of Zondervan. All rights reserved. Other versions used include: *THE MESSAGE* (MSG). Copyright © 1993, 1994, 1995, 1996, 2000, 2001, 2002. Used by permission of NavPress Publishing Group; the New King James Version (NKJV). Copyright © 1982 by Thomas Nelson, Inc. Used by permission. All rights reserved; the New American Standard Bible® (NASB), Copyright © 1960, 1962, 1963, 1968, 1971, 1972, 1973, 1975, 1977, 1995 by The Lockman Foundation. Used by permission; and the King James Version (KJV).

Printed in the United States of America

1 2 3 4 5 6 7 8 / 13 12 11 10 09

CONTENTS

ACKNOWLEDGMENTS

Many individuals contributed to this work. My wife and best friend, Darci, has been a tremendous support and resource as she became a proofreader, was a sounding board for my ideas, and took on more responsibility around the house as deadlines drew near. To me she's a living portrait of the Proverbs 31 woman!

I want to thank Ragnar Oborn, who not only introduced me to Jesus but has been a mentor and good friend since I committed my life to Jesus. During this project, Rags was a steady source of encouragement and contributed to this book in ways too numerous to count.

I also want to thank the many Navigator staff members, church leaders, and university students across Canada who were willing to test-drive this material in its infancy stages.

Thanks to my cousin Hugh Syme for graciously providing the cover design for this work. Your artistic ability is truly amazing!

I want to thank my mom for always believing in me and telling me that I could do and be whatever I put my mind to.

My kids—Benjamin, Mikaela, and Moriah—bring me unspeakable joy. Through them God has taught me so much about his unconditional love. They are amazing gifts!

Lastly, this book belongs to those of you who want to reach a dying world with the gospel message. I hope this material helps you reach out and win those within your sphere of influence!

PROGRESS REPORT

Scripture Memory

SESSION	VERSE TOPIC	VERSE LOCATION	INITIAL	DATE
1	God's Love and His Plan	John 10:10		
2	Our Problem: Separation from God	Romans 3:23		
3	God's Remedy: The Cross	1 Peter 3:18		
4	Humanity's Response	John 5:24		
5	Assurance of Salvation	1 John 5:12-13		

Bible Study

SESSION	BIBLE STUDY TITLE	INITIAL	DATE
1	God's Love and His Plan		
2	Our Problem: Separation from God		
3	God's Remedy: The Cross		
4	Humanity's Response		
5	Assurance of Salvation		
6	Living Out the Gospel		
7	Embodying the Gospel Through Community		
8	Explaining the Gospel Through Words		
9	Preparing Your Personal Testimony		
10	Bringing in the Harvest		
11	Discipling a New Believer		

Faith Steps

Session	Faith Step	Initial	Date
1	Meditated on God's love for you		
2	Imagined how you'd feel as a nonbeliever		
3	Watched a prime-time television show and reflected on its values		
4	Interviewed one person who holds a worldview different from yours		
5	Fasted for one day and completed the Acts 29 Prayer Circle in appendix C		
6	Updated your Acts 29 Prayer Circle and identified where the people listed on your Prayer Circle fall on the evangelism process scale		
7	In a practical way, served someone listed on your Acts 29 Prayer Circle		
8	Planned a social event with your small group and committed to bringing a non-Christian friend to the event		
9	Spent one day fasting and praying for the people listed on your Acts 29 Prayer Circle		
10	Shared the gospel with a non-Christian you've been praying for		
11	Spent an hour of relational time with a person listed on your Acts 29 Prayer Circle		

INTRODUCTION

ROAD MAP FOR THE INTRODUCTION

1. Pray.
2. Read over the introductory material together.
3. Go over the assignment for session 1.
4. Pray.

SESSION OBJECTIVES

1. To understand the purpose of this workbook.

2. To understand the structure of the workbook and small-group sessions.

3. To understand the format of each session.

4. To learn how to memorize a verse effectively.

FAITH AS A PROCESS

When I was ten years old, I went through an experience that rocked my world. My parents divorced. To be honest, I didn't know how to handle it, so I rebelled against everything. Before long, I found myself in the custody of the Children's Aid Society, which forced me to attend reform school for two years and live in a foster home for six months.

In high school, I began to sense that something was missing. I gave myself over to athletics and partying, thinking these activities would bring satisfaction. I got the grades I needed so I could go to college in order to play football. However, by the time I arrived at college, my partying was out of control. My life consisted of a trail of broken relationships, bar fights, and hangovers.

One evening, while my roommate and I sat in our dorm room studying, Ragnar knocked at the door. Rags, a short and stocky guy with shoulder-length hair, was from Sweden. He looked like a Viking! He asked if we wanted to attend a pizza party/Bible study in his room. Our appetites got the better of us, so we went.

After we filled up on pizza, Rags read something from the Bible and then led us in a discussion of the material. Although I showed up to satisfy my physical appetite, the pizza just didn't do it for me. I wanted something more. Once the others left, I went back to Rags's room and asked for a pocket New Testament. That year, I'd lie on my bed reading the New Testament, and when someone knocked at the door, I'd hide the Bible under my pillow because I didn't want anyone to know what I was doing.

The next year, I showed up for football training camp. My life was still pretty messy, and I hadn't arranged for a place to live. Rags invited me to stay at his place for a few days. When I got to his apartment, I noticed he had three bedrooms but only one roommate. I asked if I could just live there. Rags said that he'd need to check with his other roommate. Years later, I learned that Ragnar never asked his earthly roommate but instead spent time asking God if taking me as a roommate was the right move. Apparently, God gave Rags the green light, and the next year living in that apartment totally changed my life.

Some mornings I'd come out of my room after a night of partying, and just the sight of Ragnar would bring tremendous guilt. Rags never said anything, and he didn't send any judgmental vibes my way. Later, I realized that he just loved me and lived out his faith. Ragnar also had an entire bookshelf filled with books on the Christian faith. I devoured most of those books that year and spent countless hours, sometimes into the wee hours of the morning, talking with Ragnar about spiritual issues. At some point that year, I came to faith, and God began working on various behaviors in my life. Almost immediately, God tapped me on the shoulder about my out-of-control drinking, and he dealt with some of my other issues as well.

At the end of the year, God brought an InterVarsity staff worker into my life. Mark helped me grow in my newfound faith over the next two years. He recognized that God had given me the gift of evangelism, so he provided me ways to express that gift. Mark prayed with me, laughed with me, and handed me Kleenex as God continued the healing process in my soul.

As I look back over my story, I see a process at work. The foster home I ended up in at age ten was a Christian home. In high school, a Christian teacher said some kind words that kept me going. Then God brought Rags and Mark into my life. How long did it take me to come to faith? I guess the better part of twenty years. It took a process divinely orchestrated by a sovereign God—a God with perfect timing who brought people into the process who were the perfect people for me.

WHY THIS COURSE?

Just as my journey to faith involved a process, the same holds true with all people at all times. God works behind the scenes, orchestrating events and circumstances in order to draw individuals into a relationship with their loving and good Creator.

The purpose of this workbook is to help you understand the process and your role in it so you feel better equipped when God uses you to draw someone he loves to himself.

Of course, the danger of any course like this is seeing it as a mechanical process to work through in a linear fashion. As a result, we'll likely think that if we simply master certain techniques, we'll be effective in advancing the gospel. Clearly, life doesn't work that way. Sometimes it may even seem that people are moving one step forward and two steps back. Some might never move forward at all! Still, understanding the basics of the process can help us relate to those around us in a relevant way.

WHAT DOES "ACTS 29" MEAN?

In the New Testament, the book of Acts provides the amazing story of how the gospel spread geographically throughout the known world. In fact, at the end of Acts, the apostle Paul was living in a rented house in Rome. He didn't just live there—he was under house arrest. Yet Paul was free to welcome guests: "He welcomed everyone who came to visit. He urgently presented all matters of the Kingdom of God. He explained everything about Jesus Christ. His door was always open" (Acts 28:30-31, MSG).

Although those are the last words of the book of Acts, the story of Acts hasn't ended. It continues even now, and God has chosen us to write the remaining chapters—not with pen and paper but with the words and actions of our lives. Acts 29 is designed to help you do just that: share the good news of Jesus Christ in natural yet proven ways that feel natural to who you are and also show respect to the people around you.

HOW THE COURSE IS STRUCTURED

As you move forward in this workbook, you'll see an unusual metaphor to explain the process of talking with our friends, neighbors, coworkers, and others around us about Jesus. Both Jesus and Paul used this metaphor.

In Mark 4, Jesus explained the kingdom of heaven using the parable of the sower:

A farmer went out to sow his seed. As he was scattering the seed, some fell along the path, and the birds came and ate it up. Some fell on rocky places, where it did not have much soil. It sprang up quickly, because the soil was shallow. But when the sun came up, the plants were scorched, and they withered because they had no root. Other seed fell among thorns, which grew up and choked the plants, so that they did not bear grain. Still other seed fell on good soil. It came up, grew and produced a crop, multiplying thirty, sixty, or even a hundred times. (Mark 4:3-8)

In this parable, the seed represents the message of the gospel, given by God to "produce the fruit of the Kingdom in the soil of receptive and believing hearts."[1] The farmer represents those of us who sow the seed, while the four types of soil represent different types of people.

In 1 Corinthians, the apostle Paul addressed an issue dividing the Corinthian church:

What, after all, is Apollos? And what is Paul? Only servants, through whom you came to believe—as the Lord has assigned to each his task. I planted the seed, Apollos watered it, but God made it grow. So neither he who plants nor he who waters is anything, but only God, who makes things grow. The man who plants and the man who waters have one purpose, and each will be rewarded according to his own labor. For we are God's fellow workers; you are God's field, God's building. (1 Corinthians 3:5-9)

In this passage, Paul described those of us who have a part in sharing the gospel as common field hands and the people we minister to as the field.

In keeping with Jesus' and Paul's imagery, we'll look at four stages of farming (cultivating, sowing, harvesting, and multiplying) and relate them to the process of sharing the gospel with those around us.

FORMAT OF THE SESSIONS

Most of the eleven sessions in this workbook include the following elements:

Prayer. When I attended McMaster Divinity College, a group of us formed an evangelism team. We met each week to pray and ask God to work among the students on our university campus. During one outreach event that we spent hours praying for, we saw God answer our prayers when six people professed faith in Christ! As Paul wrote in 1 Corinthians 3:7, "Neither he who plants nor he who waters is anything, but only God, who makes things grow." Drawing people to Christ is God's work; he gives us the privilege of joining in his kingdom-building plan. Our work begins with prayer. Without prayer, our toil would be in vain.

Scripture Memory. Sometimes we think of memorizing Scripture as a chore we need to endure or a discipline we need to practice. But memorizing Bible verses and passages can actually help us move around the Bible more easily when we talk to people about Jesus. During this course, you'll commit several passages to memory. These verses will help you share "The Bridge to Life" (see appendix A). "The Bridge" provides a framework for explaining the good news of the gospel message.

Bible Study. Most weeks, a set of Bible studies will challenge you to dig into Scripture. Studying Scripture is very important because through his Word, God teaches, rebukes, corrects, and trains us in righteousness so that we can be thoroughly equipped for every good work (see 2 Timothy 3:16). These Bible study sessions include the following features:

- Each study is broken down into days (four to five days per session). Take twenty to thirty minutes to complete each day's lesson, and don't try to do multiple days in one sitting. This will help you develop a regular quiet time with God.
- The Bible studies are meant to get you to think deeply. In addition to your own times of study, expect to teach and learn from each other when you come together for group discussion.
- Each session includes Bible passages you need to refer to.
- To the right of the Bible passages, you'll find "Guiding Questions," with space for writing your answers. After the Bible passages, you'll find space for additional notes and observations.
- To the left of the Bible passages, you'll find "Key Insights." These insights provide cultural, linguistic, and theological information that can help you answer the Guiding Questions more fully.

Faith Step. The apostle James wrote, "Do not merely listen to the word, and so deceive yourselves. Do what it says" (1:22). Each week's session includes an assignment for you to carry out. The assignments start small and increase in difficulty. The goal of this course is to take you through the process of sharing your faith on a personal and practical level.

Progress Report. Because we can easily get discouraged and lose heart when we share our faith, this course asks you to select an accountability partner (your group leader will guide you through this process). Each week, your accountability partner will check that your Guiding Questions and Faith Step are complete and then listen to you recite the memory verse for the week. As you complete each component, your accountability partner will initial and date the relevant boxes on your progress report (found on pages 8–9). Of course, you'll do the same for that individual.

Group Discussion. Every week, the members of your group will have an opportunity to pray, discuss, challenge, encourage each other, and resolve any lingering questions.

Small-group experts say that groups of four to eight people are ideal for discussion, so don't be afraid to break down a larger group into smaller groups. For example, if twelve people want to complete this course together, you might want to have two or three groups rather than one.

Video Component. There is a video that goes with the Acts 29 curriculum. The video contains a teaching segment for each session. The course does not require the video in order to be effective; however, it does provide valuable teaching that fleshes out the written material.

GUIDELINES FOR EFFECTIVELY MEMORIZING SCRIPTURE[2]

1. Before you start to memorize a verse or passage, read it aloud several times.
2. Learn the topic, reference, and first phrase as a unit. After you review the topic, reference, and first phrase a few times, add the second phrase. Gradually add phrases until you know the whole verse.
3. Whenever possible, recite the verse aloud.
4. As you memorize and review the verse, think about how it applies to your life and the lives of those around you.
5. Recite the verse in this sequence:
   - TOPIC: "God is holy."
   - REFERENCE: "First Peter 1, 15 to 16."
   - VERSE(S): "Just as he who called you is holy, so be holy in all you do; for it is written: 'Be holy, because I am holy.'"
   - REFERENCE: "First Peter 1, 15 to 16."
6. The most critical element in Scripture memory is *review, review, review.* The most important time to review a verse repeatedly is right after you can quote the whole verse (topic, reference, verse, reference) without making a mistake. Review the verse at least once a day after that, preferably several times a day. The more you review, the greater your retention.
7. Don't consider a verse to be memorized simply at the point when you can quote it accurately. Review it frequently until it becomes ingrained in your memory.

ASSIGNMENT FOR SESSION 1

1. **Scripture Memory:** Familiarize yourself with step 1 of "The Bridge to Life" (see appendix A). Memorize the verse titled "God's Love and His Plan" (John 10:10).

Be ready to recite the verse at your next group meeting.

2. **Bible Study:** Complete "Session 1: Why Bother Sharing the Gospel?"

3. **Faith Step:** Many times, God's love doesn't seem personal. Regular meditation on specific Scripture passages can help change this perspective. Over the next week, spend at least ten minutes a day meditating on one of the following passages (Psalm 23; 91; 131; Isaiah 43:1-4; 49:14-16; Hosea 11:1-4; Matthew 10:29-31; Romans 8:31-39). Don't try to do anything to the passage; instead let the passage do something to you. Journal your reflections in the space provided below.

WHY BOTHER SHARING THE GOSPEL?

ROAD MAP FOR SESSION 1

1. Pray.
2. Break into pairs to review step 1 of "The Bridge to Life" (see appendix A). Recite the memory verse titled "God's Love and His Plan" (John 10:10) and check off the appropriate box on your progress report if you recite it correctly.
3. Review each other's Bible study material and check off the appropriate box on the progress report if complete.
4. Share how your time of meditating on God's love for you went. Check each other's journaling and check off the appropriate Faith Step on the progress report.
5. As a group, watch the video segment for this session.
6. With your group, work through "Session 1: Why Bother Sharing the Gospel?" Draw the video material into your discussion when it's relevant.
7. Pray.

SESSION OBJECTIVES

1. To see that God desires a love relationship with you.

2. To see that sharing our faith isn't a matter of choice but a matter of obedience and love.

3. To understand that when we obey God, he'll reveal himself to us in deeper ways.

4. To see that a deep love for God and people should be our motivation for sharing our faith.

5. To see that we'll be held accountable for whether or not we respond to God's call into mission.

PLANTING A GARDEN

Sometimes I invite my kids to help me in the garden. Of course, I know their participation will slow me down, as they move slower, are less competent, and are easily distracted. I could accomplish the work faster without my kids "helping" me, but I want them to work with me because I love them and want to spend time with them. In addition, I want them to learn, grow, and mature into the people they're capable of becoming, even through simple things like teaching them how to hold a shovel or dig a hole.

Reaching people with the gospel of Jesus is a lot like this. God knows that by involving us, the process will be slow and inefficient. Because we're so broken and needy and have so much to learn, God could easily accomplish his kingdom-building plan much faster if he went it alone! For example, he could convert people the same way he converted Paul on the road to Damascus—making a personal appearance to every person on the planet.

GOD DESIRES A LOVE RELATIONSHIP WITH US

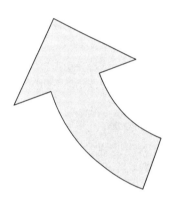

3.
Obedience leads to
deeper relationship
with God.

1.
God initiates love
relationship and
invites us into mission.

2.
We respond by
obeying or disobeying.

This diagram shows God's motivation for inviting us to participate with him in building his kingdom. Step 1 of the diagram explains that God loves us and wants us to partner with him in mission. The reason he does this is that he wants relationship.

Step 2 of the cycle explains that we have a choice — to respond in obedience to God's invitation or disobey.

Finally, step 3 shows that as we step out in obedience and engage in mission, we grow in our relationship with God and with each other because he reveals himself to us in deeper ways. Let's explore the process in more detail by looking at two biblical examples.

In Genesis 12:1-3, we catch a glimpse of God's vision for the world. Through one man, Abraham, God is going to build one nation, Israel, which will be the channel of blessing and salvation to all the nations of the earth.

> "Soul winners are not soul winners because of what they know, but because of the Person they know, how well they know Him, and how much they long for others to know Him."
>
> — Dawson Trotman, founder of The Navigators

KEY INSIGHTS	GENESIS 12:1-5	GUIDING QUESTIONS
"LEAVE YOUR COUNTRY . . . AND GO" (GENESIS 12:1) The promises to Abraham renew the vision for humanity set out in Genesis 1 and 2. He, like Noah before him, is a second Adam figure. Adam was given the garden: Abraham is promised the land of Canaan. God told Adam to be fruitful and multiply: Abraham is promised descendents as numerous as the stars in heaven. God walked with Adam in Eden: Abraham was told to walk before God. In this way the advent of Abraham is seen as the answer to the problems set out in Genesis 1-11: through him all the families of the earth will be blessed.[1]	[1]The Lord had said to Abram, "Leave your country, your people and your father's household and go to the land I will show you. [2]"I will make you into a great nation and I will bless you; I will make your name great, and you will be a blessing. [3]I will bless those who bless you, and whoever curses you I will curse; and all peoples on earth will be blessed through you." [4]So Abram left, as the Lord had told him; and Lot went with him. Abram was seventy-five years old when he set out from Haran. [5]He took his wife Sarai, his nephew Lot, all the possessions they had accumulated and the people they had acquired in Haran, and they set out for the land of Canaan, and they arrived there.	What six things does God promise Abraham in this passage? 1. 2. 3. 4. 5. 6. How do you see the love cycle present in this encounter? Phase 1: Phase 2: Phase 3: (You'll have to draw on your knowledge of the rest of Abraham's life to answer this portion.)

NOTES AND OBSERVATIONS:

DAY TWO

GOD DESIRES A LOVE RELATIONSHIP WITH US (PART 2)

In Genesis 15:13, God told Abraham that his "descendants will be strangers in a country not their own, and they will be enslaved and mistreated four hundred years." This is where the story picks up in Exodus. "God heard [the] groaning [of his people] and he remembered his covenant with Abraham" (Exodus 2:24). In response he called upon Moses to deliver his people and lead them to the Promised Land.

KEY INSIGHTS	EXODUS 3:1-14	GUIDING QUESTIONS
"MY PEOPLE THE ISRAEL-ITES" (EXODUS 3:10) [Israel] is to be a display people, a showcase to the world of how being in covenant with God changes a people.[2] **"WHO AM I?" (EXODUS 3:11)** Five times Moses tried to excuse himself from God's call (see also 3:13; 4:1,10,13). God assured Moses that he would be present during the deliverance and that the nation would one day worship God at that very mountain (3:12).[3]	[1]Now Moses was tending the flock of Jethro his father-in-law, the priest of Midian, and he led the flock to the far side of the desert and came to Horeb, the mountain of God. [2]There the angel of the Lord appeared to him in flames of fire from within a bush. Moses saw that though the bush was on fire it did not burn up. [3]So Moses thought, "I will go over and see this strange sight — why the bush does not burn up." [4]When the Lord saw that he had gone over to look, God called to him from within the bush, "Moses! Moses!" And Moses said, "Here I am." [5]"Do not come any closer," God said. "Take off your sandals, for the place where you are standing is holy ground." [6]Then he said, "I am the God of your father, the God of Abraham, the God of Isaac and the God of Jacob." At this, Moses hid his face, because he was afraid to look at God. [7]The Lord said, "I have indeed seen the misery of my people in Egypt. I have heard them crying out because of their slave drivers, and I am concerned about their suffering. [8]So I have come down to rescue them from the hand of the Egyptians and to bring them up out of that land into a good and spacious land, a land flowing with milk and honey. . . . [9]And now the cry of the Israelites has reached me, and I have seen the way the Egyptians are oppressing them. [10]So now, go. I am sending you to Pharaoh to bring my people the Israelites out of Egypt."	How do you see the love cycle present in this encounter? Phase 1: Phase 2: Phase 3: (You'll have to draw on your knowledge of the rest of Moses' life to answer this portion.) Make a list of the experiences that Moses would have missed if he hadn't obeyed God's call to mission. Would missing these experiences have made Moses better or worse? Explain your answer. Read John 14:21. What three things does Jesus promise in this passage? 1. 2.

	¹¹But Moses said to God, "Who am I, that I should go to Pharaoh and bring the Israelites out of Egypt?" ¹²And God said, "I will be with you. And this will be the sign to you that it is I who have sent you: When you have brought the people out of Egypt, you will worship God on this mountain." ¹³Moses said to God, "Suppose I go to the Israelites and say to them, 'The God of your fathers has sent me to you,' and they ask me, 'What is his name?' Then what shall I tell them?" ¹⁴God said to Moses, "I am who I am. This is what you are to say to the Israelites: 'I am has sent me to you.'"	3. How do the promises in this verse support Phase 3 of the love cycle? How did God fulfill these promises in the lives of Abraham and Moses? Pause for a moment. Can you recall any other examples of God's revealing himself to a person in Scripture and then calling him or her into mission? Can you think of any other individuals who obeyed God's call to mission? What was the result? Can you think of anyone who chose to disobey God's call to mission? What was the result? Can you think of any other biblical characters who grew in their knowledge and love for God through obeying the call to mission?

NOTES AND OBSERVATIONS:

DAY THREE

THE GREAT COMMANDMENT

In Matthew 22:34-40, a Pharisee tested Jesus by asking him, "Which is the greatest commandment?" Jesus' answer combines two texts (Deuteronomy 6:5 and Leviticus 19:18). If the main motivation for sharing our faith is a love for God and for other people, this should be a key passage in motivating us to share our faith.

KEY INSIGHTS	MATTHEW 22:34-40	GUIDING QUESTIONS
"HEART . . . SOUL . . . MIND" (MATTHEW 22:37) Heart, soul, and mind are not different "parts" of man, but different ways of thinking of the whole man in relation to God. . . . The three nouns together indicate the essential nature of man, his ultimate, fundamental loyalty, not just a superficial allegiance.[4] **"LOVE YOUR NEIGHBOR AS YOURSELF"** (MATTHEW 22:39) As *yourself* assumes, rather than commands, a basically self-centered orientation, which Jesus requires his disciples to overcome.[5]	[34]Hearing that Jesus had silenced the Sadducees, the Pharisees got together. [35]One of them, an expert in the law, tested him with this question: [36]"Teacher, which is the greatest commandment in the Law?" [37]Jesus replied: "'Love the Lord your God with all your heart and with all your soul and with all your mind.' [38]This is the first and greatest commandment. [39]And the second is like it: 'Love your neighbor as yourself.' [40]All the Law and the Prophets hang on these two commandments."	Would you say that your allegiance to God is deep or superficial? Why? How do you determine this? How do you "love" yourself? Read 1 Corinthians 13:4-7 for help. How is sharing your faith an act of love toward God and your "neighbor"?

NOTES AND OBSERVATIONS:

DAY FOUR

JESUS COMMISSIONS US TO SHARE THE GOSPEL

After the Resurrection, Jesus brings together his disciples and commissions them to continue the work he has begun. This same commission applies to us, as well. Let's look at this command as given in Luke and Acts.

KEY INSIGHTS	LUKE 24:46-49	GUIDING QUESTIONS
"WITNESSES" (LUKE 24:48) This is a word "from the justice system identifying someone called to testify to what he or she has experienced."[6] **"BE MY WITNESSES"** **(ACTS 1:8)** As Jesus had been anointed at his baptism with the Holy Spirit and power, so his followers were now to be similarly anointed and enabled to carry on his work.[7]	[46][Jesus] told them, "This is what is written: The Christ will suffer and rise from the dead on the third day, [47]and repentance and forgiveness of sins will be preached in his name to all nations, beginning at Jerusalem. [48]You are witnesses of these things. [49]I am going to send you what my Father has promised; but stay in the city until you have been clothed with power from on high." ## ACTS 1:6-8 [6]When they met together, they asked him, "Lord, are you at this time going to restore the kingdom to Israel?" [7]He said to them: "It is not for you to know the times or dates the Father has set by his own authority. [8]But you will receive power when the Holy Spirit comes on you; and you will be my witnesses in Jerusalem, and in all Judea and Samaria, and to the ends of the earth."	What four things does Jesus say that his witnesses will tell people about? 1. 2. 3. 4. What power is Jesus referring to in Luke 24:49? What things were the disciples concerning themselves with? What are some other things Christians concern themselves with? What did Jesus say we should concern ourselves with?

NOTES AND OBSERVATIONS:

DAY FIVE

PAUL AND SHARING THE GOSPEL

The apostle Paul provided a model for the proper motive for sharing the gospel. He was careful to point out that he didn't want to draw attention to himself. Instead, because of Christ's love, he evangelized ("persuades men") and did it with a "right mind" (2 Corinthians 5:11-13).

We see the evidence of Christ's love in his death and resurrection for all. As a result, we can "die" to self-centered living and fulfill the purpose of living for Christ.[8]

KEY INSIGHTS	2 CORINTHIANS 5:6-20	GUIDING QUESTIONS
"JUDGMENT SEAT OF CHRIST" (1 CORINTHIANS 5:10) "Judgment seat" comes from the Greek word *bema*. It literally means "foot-room" and was used to denote a raised place or platform, reached by steps, originally that at Athens in the Phyx Hill, where was the place of assembly; from the platform orations were made. In the Greco-Roman world, this was the place that judgments were handed down by rulers of the day (see Matthew 27:19; Acts 12:21; 18:12). The Olympic Games also used this location to hand out awards to the winning athletes. It is important to note that this "judgment seat" is not the judgment of salvation described in Revelation 20:11-15, which is referred to as the "Great White Throne of Judgment." At this judgment seat believers are to be made manifest, that each may "receive the things done in (or through) the body," according to what he has done, "whether it be good or bad." There they will receive rewards for their faithfulness to the Lord. For all that has been contrary in their lives to his will they will suffer loss (1 Corinthians 3:15).[9]	[6]We are always confident and know that as long as we are at home in the body we are away from the Lord. [7]We live by faith, not by sight. [8]We are confident, I say, and would prefer to be away from the body and at home with the Lord. [9]So we make it our goal to please him, whether we are at home in the body or away from it. [10]For we must all appear before the judgment seat of Christ, that each one may receive what is due him for the things done while in the body, whether good or bad. [11]Since, then, we know what it is to fear the Lord, we try to persuade men. What we are is plain to God, and I hope it is also plain to your conscience. [12]We are not trying to commend ourselves to you again, but are giving you an opportunity to take pride in us, so that you can answer those who take pride in what is seen rather than in what is in the heart. [13]If we are out of our mind, it is for the sake of God; if we are in our right mind, it is for you. [14]For Christ's love compels us, because we are convinced that one died for all, and therefore all died. [15]And he died for all, that those who live should no longer live for themselves but for him who died for them and was raised again. [16]So from now on we regard no one from a worldly point of view. Though we once regarded Christ in this way, we do so no longer. [17]Therefore, if anyone is in Christ, he is a new creation; the old has gone, the new has come! [18]All this is from God, who reconciled us to himself through Christ	In this passage, Paul provides at least five things that motivated him to be engaged in evangelism. What are they? Highlight or underline them. Do you think these are good motives for evangelism? Why or why not? Which of the five would motivate you the most?

	and gave us the ministry of reconciliation: [19]that God was reconciling the world to himself in Christ, not counting men's sins against them. And he has committed to us the message of reconciliation. [20]We are therefore Christ's ambassadors, as though God were making his appeal through us. We implore you on Christ's behalf: Be reconciled to God.	

NOTES AND OBSERVATIONS:

ASSIGNMENT FOR SESSION 2

1. **Scripture Memory:** Review steps 1 and 2 of "The Bridge to Life" (see appendix A) and memorize the verse titled "Our Problem: Separation from God" (Romans 3:23). Be ready to recite it during your next group meeting.
2. **Bible Study:** Complete "Session 2: The Process of Evangelism."
3. **Faith Step:** In order to understand something of the despair felt by people who don't follow Jesus, try to imagine that you don't believe in God. How would you feel differently about yourself? About other people? About the future? About right and wrong? Journal your thoughts here and be prepared to share your thoughts the next time you meet with your group.

MEMORY VERSE

God's Love and His Plan

"I have come that they may have life, and have it to the full."

—JOHN 10:10

THE PROCESS OF EVANGELISM

ROAD MAP FOR SESSION 2

1. Pray.
2. Break into pairs to review step 2 of "The Bridge to Life." Recite the memory verse titled "Our Problem: Separation from God" (Romans 3:23) and check off the appropriate box on your progress report if you recite it correctly.
3. Review each other's Bible study material and check off the appropriate box on the progress report if complete.
4. Share your Faith Step reflection exercise from session 1 and check off the appropriate box on the progress report if complete.
5. As a group, watch the video segment for this session.
6. With your group, work through "Session 2: The Process of Evangelism." Draw the video material into your discussion when it's relevant.
7. Pray.

SESSION OBJECTIVES

1. To see the importance of understanding that reaching others for Christ is a process rather than an event.

2. To understand the process.

3. To understand our roles in the process.

4. To gain practice in identifying the different stages of the process.

GOD IS IN CONTROL

When I returned home from college, I was eager to share my newfound faith with my family and friends. In my mind, I equated the idea of reaching others for Christ with reaping—the part of the process in which you "close the deal" and convince the other person to ask Jesus to be Savior.

But my brother, Tyler, was like an uncultivated field. The unproductive ground of his life needed to be broken up before I could even think about reaping. At first, Tyler saw my faith in Christ as just a phase. "He'll get over it," he'd say to other family members. But as time went on, Tyler began to see changes taking place in my life. I did my best to love him unconditionally and pray for him continuously. Eventually, he was ready to listen to me talk about the message of the gospel. And after ten years, Tyler submitted to Christ!

I finally saw the harvest, but it was a long process. I realized that when anyone comes to Christ, it will always be the result of a process. I could have given up on my brother, convincing myself that he was just poor soil—an unproductive place to try to plant the seeds of the gospel. But the truth is that God was working in Tyler's life—the whole time. And God's timing was perfect.

THE PROCESS OF REACHING OTHERS FOR CHRIST

The Bible often uses agricultural metaphors to teach us about evangelism. Let's look at some of these metaphors to help us understand the process of reaching others for Christ, as well as our place in that process.

DAY ONE

SOWING THE SEED

In Mark 4:1-34, we find three parables that relate to growth: the sower (see verses 3-8), the growing seed (see verses 26-29), and the mustard seed (see verses 30-32). Each parable reflects on sowing, growth, and harvest elements that illustrate the character of the coming of the kingdom of God proclaimed by Jesus.[1] Let's explore how two of these parables compare the process of evangelism to the process of farming.

KEY INSIGHTS	MARK 4:1-20	GUIDING QUESTIONS
"TAUGHT THEM . . . BY PARABLES" (MARK 4:2) The parable of the sower accurately reflects farming life in first-century Palestine, when plowing followed sowing. The farmer wasn't being careless when he scattered seed on the path or among the thorns or on the ground where the soil was shallow. He did so intentionally, knowing he'd plow the fallow ground to receive the seed.[2] **"GREW AND PRODUCED A CROP" (MARK 4:8)** The harvest served as a common symbol for the completion of God's Kingdom. The parable of the sower includes significant reflection on the future aspect of the Kingdom, including that it will be glorious in character. In addition, the parable also reflects on activity prior to the harvest, the sowing of the seed and its growth.[3]	[1]Again Jesus began to teach by the lake. The crowd that gathered around him was so large that he got into a boat and sat in it out on the lake, while all the people were along the shore at the water's edge. [2]He taught them many things by parables, and in his teaching said: [3]"Listen! A farmer went out to sow his seed. [4]As he was scattering the seed, some fell along the path, and the birds came and ate it up. [5]Some fell on rocky places, where it did not have much soil. It sprang up quickly, because the soil was shallow. [6]But when the sun came up, the plants were scorched, and they withered because they had no root. [7]Other seed fell among thorns, which grew up and choked the plants, so that they did not bear grain. [8]Still other seed fell on good soil. It came up, grew and produced a crop, multiplying thirty, sixty, or even a hundred times. " [9]Then Jesus said, "He who has ears to hear, let him hear." [10]When he was alone, the Twelve and the others around him asked him about the parables. [11]He told them, "The secret of the kingdom of God has been given to you. But to those on the outside everything is said in parables [12]so that, 'they may be ever seeing but never perceiving, and ever	What do the farmer, the seed, and the soil symbolize in the parable of the sower? What is significant about each of these three elements in the parable? Farmer: Seed: Soil: What process do you see present in this parable?

"THE SOIL PRODUCES GRAIN" (MARK 4:28)

The parable of the sower focuses on the resistance and obstruction encountered by the seed. By contrast, the parable of the growing seed emphasizes the power released through the scattering of the seed, as well as the connection between the sower and the harvester.[4]

hearing but never understanding; otherwise they might turn and be forgiven!'"

[13]Then Jesus said to them, "Don't you understand this parable? How then will you understand any parable? [14]The farmer sows the word. [15]Some people are like seed along the path, where the word is sown. As soon as they hear it, Satan comes and takes away the word that was sown in them. [16]Others, like seed sown on rocky places, hear the word and at once receive it with joy. [17]But since they have no root, they last only a short time. When trouble or persecution comes because of the word, they quickly fall away. [18]Still others, like seed sown among thorns, hear the word; [19]but the worries of this life, the deceitfulness of wealth and the desires for other things come in and choke the word, making it unfruitful. [20]Others, like seed sown on good soil, hear the word, accept it, and produce a crop — thirty, sixty or even a hundred times what was sown."

MARK 4:26-29

[26]He also said, "This is what the kingdom of God is like. A man scatters seed on the ground. [27]Night and day, whether he sleeps or gets up, the seed sprouts and grows, though he does not know how. [28]All by itself the soil produces grain — first the stalk, then the head, then the full kernel in the head. [29]As soon as the grain is ripe, he puts the sickle to it, because the harvest has come."

What does this parable teach about sharing the gospel with others?

Compare the parable of the growing seed with the parable of the sower. How are they similar? How are they different?

How does this comparison help you understand the process of sowing, plowing, growing, and harvesting when sharing your faith with others?

NOTES AND OBSERVATIONS:

MORE TEACHING ON THE PROCESS

DAY TWO

In 1 Corinthians 3, the apostle Paul addressed divisions within the Corinthian church. These divisions were a result of the people being worldly. The solution to regaining unity comes from a proper understanding of spiritual truth. In verses 5-9, Paul used agricultural imagery to explain that these early Christians shouldn't be claiming allegiance to Paul or Apollos or anyone else except God.

KEY INSIGHTS	1 CORINTHIANS 3:5-9	GUIDING QUESTIONS
"GOD, WHO MAKES THINGS GROW" (1 CORINTHIANS 3:7) That the earth may bring forth fruit, there is need of ploughing and sowing, and other means of culture; but after all this has been carefully done, the husbandman's labour would be of no avail, did not the Lord from heaven *give the increase*, by the breaking forth of the sun, and still more by his wonderful and secret influence.[5]	[5]What, after all, is Apollos? And what is Paul? Only servants, through whom you came to believe — as the Lord has assigned to each his task. [6]I planted the seed, Apollos watered it, but God made it grow. [7]So neither he who plants nor he who waters is anything, but only God, who makes things grow. [8]The man who plants and the man who waters have one purpose, and each will be rewarded according to his own labor. [9]For we are God's fellow workers; you are God's field, God's building.	What stages of the process of evangelism are outlined in this passage? Who is responsible for: Planting Watering Growth

```
┌────────────────────────────────────────┐
│        NOTES AND OBSERVATIONS:          │
│                                          │
│                                          │
│                                          │
│                                          │
└────────────────────────────────────────┘
```

In John 4, Jesus stopped at a well and asked a Samaritan woman for a drink. This led quite naturally to a spiritual conversation with her that included agricultural metaphors. After she left, Jesus seized the time alone to teach his disciples about sharing their faith.

KEY INSIGHTS	JOHN 4:35-38	GUIDING QUESTIONS
"HE HAD TO GO THROUGH SAMARIA" (JOHN 4:4) Typically, Jewish people avoided Samaria because they despised the Samaritan people. However, Jesus intentionally went through Samaria because he wanted to witness to these people.	35"Do you not say, 'Four months more and then the harvest'? I tell you, open your eyes and look at the fields! They are ripe for harvest. 36Even now the reaper draws his wages, even now he harvests the crop for eternal life, so that the sower and the reaper may be glad together. 37Thus the saying 'One sows and another reaps' is true. 38I sent you to reap what you have not worked for. Others have done the hard work, and you have reaped the benefits of their labor."	Who do you think "others" are in this passage? What evidence in this passage do you see of a process? What implications does this passage have for the way you view sharing your faith?

NOTES AND OBSERVATIONS:

MAKING THE PROCESS PRACTICAL

DAY THREE

The passages we've studied so far show us the process of reaching others for Christ. Sometimes this process happens quickly, but often it takes considerable time—even years!

> "Conversion is a process. . . . Every time a person confronts an obstacle, it's decision time. Few of us make it in one big decision. Instead, it's a multitude of small choices — mini-decisions that a person makes toward Christ."
>
> — Jim Petersen,
> *Living Proof*

God often uses many people, circumstances, and events to bring someone to himself. He might use you to accomplish only part of the task. Perhaps you cultivate, but then the friend you're talking about spiritual issues with moves to another city. God is sovereign and can use other influences to bring that person the rest of the way. At other times, God might use you to accomplish the entire process. The important thing is to trust him!

When we understand that evangelism is a process, we benefit in many ways. First, our expectations line up with reality. If we think that most people will come to faith immediately after we share the gospel, we'll easily become discouraged and lose heart when they don't. However, if we see reaching friends, family members, neighbors, and others as a process, we mentally and spiritually prepare ourselves to enter into that process for an indefinite period of time.

Second, a proper understanding of this process helps us meet people right where they are. We don't want to verbally explain the gospel message when someone needs practical help or to be served (for example, needing groceries in the cupboards or prayer for a sick spouse or child). At the same time, we don't want to be only serving someone who is ready to receive Christ. We don't want to try to verbally explain the gospel when a person needs cultivating, but we also don't want to spend time cultivating when a person is ready to receive Christ.

In addition, we need to be careful not to treat people like projects. Every individual you know or meet has been created in God's image. Everything you learn as you complete this workbook merely provides tools to help you reach people you love who aren't yet following Jesus.

The following chart illustrates the process of evangelism. Always keep in mind that God is sovereign over the entire process. God might limit our role sometimes, yet he invites us into his mission because he wants to be in relationship with us and wants us to grow and mature. Spend some time studying the chart closely.

In order to put this chart to practical use, spend some time practicing figuring out where people sit on the process scale. Listed here are several examples of biblical characters who encountered either Jesus or his followers. Read the Scripture passage and identify where you think each person sits on the process scale. Circle the number on the scale below each individual or group. You might want to make notes in the margins so you can explain your answers in your small group.

The People of the Region of Gadarenes (Matthew 8:28-34)
-6 -5 -4 -3 -2 -1 1 2 3 4 5 6

The Rich Young Ruler (Matthew 19:16-26)
-6 -5 -4 -3 -2 -1 1 2 3 4 5 6

Nicodemus (John 3:1-21)
-6 -5 -4 -3 -2 -1 1 2 3 4 5 6

The Samaritan Woman (John 4:1-42)
-6 -5 -4 -3 -2 -1 1 2 3 4 5 6

The Process of Evangelism Chart[6]

PHASE	CULTIVATION	SOWING	HARVESTING	MULTIPLICATION
Metaphor	The Soil	The Seed	The Grain	New Crop
Human Equivalent	The Heart	The Word of God	New Life in Christ	Spiritual Reproduction
Application	Breaks up the fallow ground through relationship	Enacts the gospel through life, communicates the gospel through words, and embodies the gospel through community	Encourages a sincere decision to submit to Christ's lordship	New life begets new life in those within our sphere of influence
Emphasis	Presence of believer or community of believers in the life of the individual, focusing on building bridges of trust and respect through relationship	Present the truth of the gospel by enacting it in your life, explaining it with your words, and embodying it in community	Persuade person to make a decision to submit to Christ's lordship	Reproduce new life in the lives of others; at this point, the process begins all over again
Obstacles	Indifference Rebellion Ignorance	Ignorance Error	Love of darkness Indecision	Lack of training Isolation Lack of vision Self-centeredness

Process Scale	-6	-5	-4	-3	-2	-1	1	2	3	4	5	6
Mini Steps Leading to Conversion	Indifference or hostility toward Christ	Aware of Christian's presence	Interested in Christ	Sees and hears message	Understands implications of message	Has positive attitude toward Christ	Recognizes personal need	Repents/believes/receives	New life in Christ	Is discipled in Christian life	Is equipped to minister	Reproduces spiritual life

DAY FOUR

ADDITIONAL PRACTICE

Continue your practice of identifying where certain biblical characters stand on the process scale from page 32. Read each Scripture passage and circle the number on the scale that indicates where you think that individual or group belongs on the process scale. Again, be prepared to explain your answers in your small group.

Pilate (John 18:28-40)

-6   -5   -4   -3   -2   -1   1   2   3   4   5   6

The Ethiopian Eunuch (Acts 8:26-40)

-6   -5   -4   -3   -2   -1   1   2   3   4   5   6

Saul (Acts 9)

-6   -5   -4   -3   -2   -1   1   2   3   4   5   6

The Epicurean and Stoic Philosophers (Acts 17:16-34)

-6   -5   -4   -3   -2   -1   1   2   3   4   5   6

Felix (Acts 24)

-6   -5   -4   -3   -2   -1   1   2   3   4   5   6

Before your small group meets again, spend some time thinking about the practical use of identifying where people you know are on the process scale. Provide at least two reasons why this is beneficial and be prepared to discuss them with the rest of your group.

MEMORY VERSE

Our Problem: Separation from God

"For all have sinned and fall short of the glory of God."
—ROMANS 3:23

ASSIGNMENT FOR SESSION 3

1. **Scripture Memory:** Review steps 1 and 2 of "The Bridge to Life" (see appendix A) and memorize the verse titled "God's Remedy: The Cross" (1 Peter 3:18). Be ready to recite it during your next group meeting.

2. **Bible Study:** Complete "Session 3: Understanding People and Their Culture."

3. **Faith Step:** Before the next meeting of your group, watch a prime-time television show (including commercials). If possible, watch with someone who isn't a Christian. In fact, try to watch that person's favorite show. By doing so, you can build your relationship and be a student of culture at the same time. As you watch, answer the following questions. Be prepared to share your answers the next time your group meets.

   • What do the characters in the show value?

   • What would be their response to the question "What is the meaning of life?"

   • Think about the commercials. What do the sponsors feel you need or value?

"It seems that before we sow the word, we need to break up the unplowed ground, dig out the rocks, and uproot the thorns. If the soil is a human heart, then we need to cultivate that heart, clearing out obstacles and preparing it to receive the word. This is cultivation. Only when cultivation is well underway do we sow the Word, continuing our cultivating all along. When the word produces spiritual birth in the person's heart, we can harvest that crop — a new believer. But we don't just hide the harvest in a barn; we equip and send the new believer to multiply, bearing fruit in other's lives."

— K. C. Hinckley, *Living Proof: A Small Group Discussion Guide*

ACTS 29

"You've had your chance. The non-Jewish outsiders are next on the list. And believe me, they're going to receive it with open arms!" Paul lived for two years in his rented house. He welcomed everyone who came to visit. He urgently presented all matters of the kingdom of God. He explained everything about Jesus Christ. His door was always open.

STAGE 1

CULTIVATING

UNDERSTANDING PEOPLE AND THEIR CULTURE

ROAD MAP FOR SESSION 3

1. Pray.
2. Break into pairs and recite the memory verse titled "God's Remedy: The Cross" (1 Peter 3:18) and check off the appropriate box on your progress report if you recite it correctly.
3. Review each other's Bible study material and check off the appropriate box on the progress report if complete.
4. Share what you learned from watching a prime-time television show.
5. As a group, watch the video segment for this session.
6. With your group, work through "Session 3: Understanding People and Their Culture." Draw the video material into your discussion when it's relevant.
7. Pray.

SESSION OBJECTIVES

1. To show that a proper understanding of people is important when sharing our faith.

2. To show that a proper understanding of culture is important when sharing our faith.

3. To gain an understanding of people and culture.

GETTING TO KNOW YOU

While working on my master of divinity degree, I managed various student residences as a way to generate income as well as share the gospel. The first year, I ran a residence of 101 males. During that year, I wanted to really get to know these guys and their culture. I started by watching the TV shows they watched, listening to music they liked, and just hanging out with them.

When it came to TV, *The Jerry Springer Show* was "the thing." Every weekday, there was standing room only in the TV lounge. *The Jerry Springer Show* is an internationally known tabloid talk show on which dysfunctional families discuss their problems before a studio audience. The episodes focus on such topics as adultery, bestiality, divorce, homosexuality, incest, pedophilia, and racism.[1] Personally, I despised this show, as its success seemed to be based on the exploitation of other people's misfortune. But I watched in the hope that I'd learn something about student culture.

One day, during a commercial, I turned to the guy sitting beside me and asked, "What is it about this show that makes it so popular?"

I'll never forget his response: "I watch it because it makes me feel better about myself. I'm not nearly as messed up as the people on this show."

The music I listened to and the conversations I had that year confirmed what I had suspected about these students: Many had a deep sense of hopelessness, hurt, and despair. More than 50 percent of their parents had divorced, and they saw institutions such as government and religion as untrustworthy.

Not surprisingly, the students placed the highest value on friendship and freedom. So that's what I focused on with the guys in that residence. I joined them for games of snow football, discussions in their rooms, and video games.

After about four months of getting to know these guys, I decided to host a gathering in my apartment, where I told them my own story of relying on the message and truth of the Bible. I invited all 101 residents, and more than sixty of them attended!

That year, I learned the importance of understanding people and their culture. So often when we want to share the gospel, we come with a prepackaged presentation or agenda and don't know anything about the other person. The old saying is true: "People don't care how much you know until they know how much you care."

WHO ARE YOU?

Let's take a shortcut in our efforts to understand people. If we want to be effective communicators for the kingdom of God, we need to understand three basic factors that shape people and how they relate to one another. Two of these factors are consistent and don't change over time. The third distinguishes the people of one generation or culture from those of another.

The three basic factors are:

1. People are created in God's image.
2. People are fallen (meaning they are sinners).
3. People are influenced by their culture.[2]

In some ways, sharing your faith is similar to being a doctor. The job of a physician is to know about the human body and how it functions when healthy. With this knowledge, a physician compares a patient's current condition with the norm and makes a diagnosis. The doctor can then propose a course of action to treat the condition.

Similarly, if you know what it means to be spiritually healthy, you can compare a friend's current condition with the norm and make a diagnosis. The diagnosis then leads to seeking a remedy.

Genesis 1–2 provides us with a picture of people before the Fall living in shalom. *Shalom*, the Hebrew word for *peace*, refers to the rich, integrated, relational wholeness that God desires for us. This is the way God intended for us to live, and it's the norm that we can measure our current situation against.

Then, in Genesis 3, God provided a diagnosis of the problem and showed us some of the symptoms. Thankfully, God doesn't leave us to our own devices for curing these symptoms; he graciously introduced a course of action to treat our condition.

> "The gospel is addressed to human beings, to their minds and hearts and consciences, and calls for a response. Human beings only exist as members of communities which share a common language, customs, ways of ordering economic and social life, ways of understanding and coping with their world. If the gospel is to be understood, if it is to be received as something which communicates truth about the real human situation, if it is, as we say, to 'make sense,' it has to be communicated in the language of those to whom it is addressed and has to be clothed in symbols which are meaningful to them."
>
> —Lesslie Newbigin, *The Gospel in a Pluralist Society*

These three chapters of Genesis provide us with invaluable insight into the makeup of people. This insight can help us share the gospel in a way that's meaningful and relevant to their lives.

PEOPLE ARE CREATED IN GOD'S IMAGE

DAY ONE

KEY INSIGHTS	GENESIS 1:26–2:9,15-25	GUIDING QUESTIONS
"IN OUR IMAGE" (GENESIS 1:26) Just as powerful earthly kings, to indicate their claim to dominion, erect an image of themselves in the provinces of their empire where they do not personally appear; so man is placed upon earth in God's image as God's sovereign emblem. He is really only God's representative, summoned to maintain and enforce God's claim to dominion over the earth. The decisive thing about man's similarity to God, therefore, is his function in the nonhuman world.[3] **"GOD . . . SAID TO THEM" (GENESIS 1:28)** Unique among the creatures, which God creates, humankind is personal. God addresses only the man and woman: they enjoy a uniquely personal relationship with God. As Augustine observed long ago in his *Confessions*, we are made for God, and our hearts are restless until we find our rest in him.[4] **"I GIVE . . . FOOD" (GENESIS 1:30)** God's provision of food for newly created man stands in sharp contrast to Mesopotamian views which held that man was created to supply the gods with food.[5]	[26]Then God said, "Let us make man in our image, in our likeness, and let them rule over the fish of the sea and the birds of the air, over the livestock, over all the earth, and over all the creatures that move along the ground." [27]So God created man in his own image, in the image of God he created him; male and female he created them. [28]God blessed them and said to them, "Be fruitful and increase in number; fill the earth and subdue it. Rule over the fish of the sea and the birds of the air and over every living creature that moves on the ground." [29]Then God said, "I give you every seed-bearing plant on the face of the whole earth and every tree that has fruit with seed in it. They will be yours for food. [30]And to all the beasts of the earth and all the birds of the air and all the creatures that move on the ground — everything that has the breath of life in it — I give every green plant for food." And it was so. [31]God saw all that he had made, and it was very good. And there was evening, and there was morning — the sixth day. [1]Thus the heavens and the earth were completed in all their vast array. [2]By the seventh day God had finished the work he had been doing; so on the seventh day he rested from all his work. [3]And God blessed the seventh day and made it holy, because on it he rested from all the work of creating that he had done. [4]This is the account of the heavens and the earth when they were created.	What does this passage teach us about the intended purpose and role of humanity? (Genesis 1:26,28; 2:15,19-20) Reread Genesis 1:26. What do you think it means for human beings to be created in the "image" and "likeness" of God? What are some ways human beings are "like" God? What are some of the differences between God and humanity?

When the Lord God made the earth and the heavens — [5]and no shrub of the field had yet appeared on the earth and no plant of the field had yet sprung up, for the Lord God had not sent rain on the earth and there was no man to work the ground, [6]but streams came up from the earth and watered the whole surface of the ground — [7]the Lord God formed the man from the dust of the ground and breathed into his nostrils the breath of life, and the man became a living being.

[8]Now the Lord God had planted a garden in the east, in Eden; and there he put the man he had formed. [9]And the Lord God made all kinds of trees grow out of the ground — trees that were pleasing to the eye and good for food. In the middle of the garden were the tree of life and the tree of the knowledge of good and evil. . . .

[15]The Lord God took the man and put him in the Garden of Eden to work it and take care of it. [16]And the Lord God commanded the man, "You are free to eat from any tree in the garden; [17]but you must not eat from the tree of the knowledge of good and evil, for when you eat of it you will surely die."

[18]The Lord God said, "It is not good for the man to be alone. I will make a helper suitable for him."

[19]Now the Lord God had formed out of the ground all the beasts of the field and all the birds of the air. He brought them to the man to see what he would name them; and whatever the man called each living creature, that was its name. [20]So the man gave names to all the livestock, the birds of the air and all the beasts of the field.

But for Adam no suitable helper was found. [21]So the Lord God caused the man to fall into a deep sleep; and while he was sleeping, he took one of the man's ribs and closed up the place with flesh. [22]Then the Lord God made a woman from the rib he had taken out of the man, and he brought her to the man.

What common beliefs in your culture contradict the teachings of Genesis 1–2 (such as the origin of humanity, our purpose, the purposes of other created things)? How does this hinder or help you in sharing your faith?

How does knowing that you are made in God's image and given a purpose and a role affect the way you share your faith with the people in your sphere of influence?

	[23]The man said, "This is now bone of my bones and flesh of my flesh; she shall be called 'woman,' for she was taken out of man."	
	[24]For this reason a man will leave his father and mother and be united to his wife, and they will become one flesh.	
	[25]The man and his wife were both naked, and they felt no shame.	

NOTES AND OBSERVATIONS:

PEOPLE ARE FALLEN

DAY TWO

Something is fundamentally wrong with the world, but what causes this? Genesis 3 identifies the fundamental problem as sin.

KEY INSIGHTS	GENESIS 3:1-24	GUIDING QUESTIONS
"YOU WILL DIE" (GENESIS 3:3) *Thanatos* (death) is used in scripture of: (a) the separation of the soul (the spiritual part of man) from the body (the material part), the latter ceasing to function and turning to dust; and (b) the separation of man from God; Adam died on the day he disobeyed God (Genesis 2:17), and hence all mankind are born in the same spiritual condition (Romans 5:12, 14,17,21).[6] **"YOU WILL BE LIKE GOD" (GENESIS 3:5)** I have no doubt that Satan promises them divinity; as if he had	[1]Now the serpent was more crafty than any of the wild animals the Lord God had made. He said to the woman, "Did God really say, 'You must not eat from any tree in the garden'?" [2]The woman said to the serpent, "We may eat fruit from the trees in the garden, [3]but God did say, 'You must not eat fruit from the tree that is in the middle of the garden, and you must not touch it, or you will die.'" [4]"You will not surely die," the serpent said to the woman. [5]"For God knows that when you eat of it your eyes will be opened, and you will be like God, knowing good and evil." [6]When the woman saw that the fruit of	What was the fundamental temptation Adam and Eve faced (see Genesis 3:5)? In what ways does this temptation still exist today? How can you use this insight in sharing your faith?

said, "For no other reason does God defraud you of the tree of knowledge, than because he fears to have you as companions."[7]

Though Adam and Eve flee from him, God graciously takes the initiative to seek them out. In declaring judgment, God curses the serpent and promises to put enmity between the serpent's offspring and that of the woman (Genesis 3:15). The woman's offspring will crush the serpent's head: God promises to extinguish the evil forces Adam and Eve have unleashed. This is the first biblical promise of the Gospel: Christ is to be "the seed of the woman" and will defeat Satan, though at great cost to himself, in the "wounding" of his "heel."[8]

the tree was good for food and pleasing to the eye, and also desirable for gaining wisdom, she took some and ate it. She also gave some to her husband, who was with her, and he ate it. [7]Then the eyes of both of them were opened, and they realized they were naked; so they sewed fig leaves together and made coverings for themselves.

[8]Then the man and his wife heard the sound of the Lord God as he was walking in the garden in the cool of the day, and they hid from the Lord God among the trees of the garden. [9]But the Lord God called to the man, "Where are you?"

[10]He answered, "I heard you in the garden, and I was afraid because I was naked; so I hid."

[11]And he said, "Who told you that you were naked? Have you eaten from the tree that I commanded you not to eat from?"

[12]The man said, "The woman you put here with me — she gave me some fruit from the tree, and I ate it."

[13]Then the Lord God said to the woman, "What is this you have done?"

The woman said, "The serpent deceived me, and I ate."

[14]So the Lord God said to the serpent, "Because you have done this, Cursed are you above all the livestock and all the wild animals! You will crawl on your belly and you will eat dust all the days of your life. [15]And I will put enmity between you and the woman, and between your offspring and hers; he will crush your head, and you will strike his heel."

[16]To the woman he said,

"I will greatly increase your pains in childbearing; with pain you will give birth to children. Your desire will be for your husband, and he will rule over you."

[17]To Adam he said, "Because you listened to your wife and ate from the tree about

From this passage, list the symptoms of sin. Then summarize each symptom in a word or two here.

1.

2.

3.

4.

5.

Which of these symptoms gives you the most trouble?

Which of these symptoms do the people you want to reach for Christ display the most?

which I commanded you, 'You must not eat of it,' Cursed is the ground because of you; through painful toil you will eat of it all the days of your life. [18]It will produce thorns and thistles for you, and you will eat the plants of the field. [19]By the sweat of your brow you will eat your food until you return to the ground, since from it you were taken; for dust you are and to dust you will return."

[20]Adam named his wife Eve, because she would become the mother of all the living.

[21]The Lord God made garments of skin for Adam and his wife and clothed them. [22]And the Lord God said, "The man has now become like one of us, knowing good and evil. He must not be allowed to reach out his hand and take also from the tree of life and eat, and live forever." [23]So the Lord God banished him from the Garden of Eden to work the ground from which he had been taken. [24]After he drove the man out, he placed on the east side of the Garden of Eden cherubim and a flaming sword flashing back and forth to guard the way to the tree of life.

How can this knowledge help you when sharing your faith?

NOTES AND OBSERVATIONS:

PEOPLE ARE INFLUENCED BY THEIR CULTURE

DAY THREE

Culture is defined as the "customs and civilization of a particular time or people."[9] We simply can't deny that people are influenced by their culture or that this influence shapes their view of the world and how they fit into that world. Quite logically, this view of the world is called a "worldview."

God knows that people are influenced by their culture. Even in ancient times, he warned the Israelites upon entering the Promised Land not to be influenced by other cultures: "You must not do as they do in Egypt, where you used to live, and you must not do as they do in the land of Canaan, where I am bringing you" (Leviticus 18:3). With the same concern, the apostle Paul later warned Christians in Rome to "not conform any longer to the pattern of this world" (Romans 12:2).

Culture doesn't exist only in ancient times or in other parts of the world. In today's world, many countries are culturally diverse. For example, Toronto, Canada, might be the most culturally diverse city in the world. More than half of Toronto's two million people are from abroad! In addition, even within a particular culture, subcultures exist. Most of us are aware of culture that is centered around age, income, music, geography, sports, and so on.

If we want God to use us to reach the people around us, we can't ignore the influence of culture. In fact, we need to understand culture's influence so we can better understand the people who call that culture home.

UNDERSTANDING A PERSON'S WORLDVIEW

God created all of us to be in relationship with him. In Ecclesiastes, we read, "[God] has also set eternity in the hearts of men" (Ecclesiastes 3:11). In light of this, we shouldn't be surprised that people who don't have a personal relationship with Christ have an insatiable desire to find fulfillment and meaning in life. Because they don't know Christ, they try to fill the void in their lives with other worldviews or philosophies. Everyone has a worldview, whether or not he or she is aware of it.

To understand someone else's worldview, we need to ask that person four basic questions:

1. Where are we? What kind of world do we live in?
2. Who are we? What does it mean to be human?
3. What's wrong? What's the fundamental problem with the world?
4. What's the remedy? What will fix the problem?[10]

The worldview we hold affects every facet of life. The following diagram illustrates the interrelationship of worldview and culture. Study the diagram and answer the questions that follow.

Often we try to change what others believe in the outer bubbles. We try to convince them that premarital sex is wrong or that abortion is wrong or that cheating on your taxes is wrong. We might be correct about the right or wrong of these points, but that's not the issue we need to address.

The center bubble (worldview) informs the surrounding bubbles. For example, if evolution forms someone's worldview, then his beliefs about the other bubbles will flow out of that core belief system. Getting at the core bubble can help us understand why people think the way they do. Once we get a grasp on an individual's worldview, then we can begin to address the most important questions: "Who is Jesus?" and "What does he want from me?"

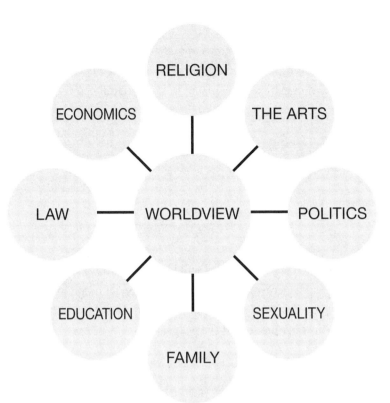

Application

- Choose one category from the worldview diagram and explain how a non-Christian worldview would influence that category. For example, how might an atheist's worldview influence his or her understanding of sexuality?

- What are some ways a person's worldview might be a barrier to hearing the message of the gospel?

- How can understanding the nature and worldview of others help us share the gospel with them?

• Once we understand the worldview of others, we can interact with them in more relevant ways. We can ask questions about their beliefs, which often results in their asking us about our beliefs. Provide an example of how you could use your understanding of culture and people to guide a friendly conversation toward spiritual matters.

PAUL AND PEOPLE OF OTHER CULTURES

While some of the people you interact with will have a religious background, others won't. In Acts 17, Paul addressed a crowd who didn't have a biblical religious heritage. Although this passage doesn't provide a model for all situations, it does show that Paul was aware of and sensitive to culture when he shared the gospel.

KEY INSIGHTS	ACTS 17:16-34	GUIDING QUESTIONS
"ATHENS" (ACTS 17:16) Although Athens had long since lost the political eminence that was hers in an earlier day, she continued to represent the highest level of culture attained in classical antiquity. The sculpture, literature, and oratory of Athens in the fifth and fourth centuries BC have, indeed, never been surpassed. In philosophy, too, she occupied the leading place, being the native city of Socrates and Plato and the adopted home of Aristotle, Epicurus, and Zeno. In all these fields Athens retained unchallenged prestige, and her political glory as the cradle of democracy was not completely dimmed. In consideration of her splendid past, the Romans gave Athens the right to maintain her own institutions as a free and allied city within the Roman Empire.[11]	[16]While Paul was waiting for them in Athens, he was greatly distressed to see that the city was full of idols. [17]So he reasoned in the synagogue with the Jews and the God-fearing Greeks, as well as in the marketplace day by day with those who happened to be there. [18]A group of Epicurean and Stoic philosophers began to dispute with him. Some of them asked, "What is this babbler trying to say?" Others remarked, "He seems to be advocating foreign gods." They said this because Paul was preaching the good news about Jesus and the resurrection. [19]Then they took him and brought him to a meeting of the Areopagus, where they said to him, "May we know what this new teaching is that you are presenting? [20]You are bringing some strange ideas to our ears, and we want to know what they mean." [21](All the Athenians and the foreigners who lived there spent their time doing nothing but talking about and listening to the latest ideas.) [22]Paul then stood up in the meeting of the Areopagus and said: "Men of Athens! I see that in every way you are very religious. [23]For as I walked around and looked carefully at your objects of worship, I even found	Highlight or underline verses in this passage that demonstrate how Paul was informed about and sensitive to Greek culture. Why do you think Paul began his sermon with the words found in Acts 17:22-23?

"VERY RELIGIOUS" (ACTS 17:22)

This Greek word could mean "pious" in a good sense or "superstitious" in a bad sense. Paul's audience would have to listen to find out whether he was being complimentary, critical, or ironic.[12]

"SOME OF YOUR OWN POETS" (ACTS 17:28)

"In him we live and move and have our being" was written by the Cretan poet Epimenides. "We are his offspring" is found in works by both Aratus and Cleanthes. All of these poets were popular with the Stoics, who understood God in their poems to be the Logos — divine Reason, the world-soul.[13]

an altar with this inscription: to an unknown god. Now what you worship as something unknown I am going to proclaim to you.

24"The God who made the world and everything in it is the Lord of heaven and earth and does not live in temples built by hands. 25And he is not served by human hands, as if he needed anything, because he himself gives all men life and breath and everything else. 26From one man he made every nation of men, that they should inhabit the whole earth; and he determined the times set for them and the exact places where they should live. 27God did this so that men would seek him and perhaps reach out for him and find him, though he is not far from each one of us. 28'For in him we live and move and have our being.' As some of your own poets have said, 'We are his offspring.'

29"Therefore since we are God's offspring, we should not think that the divine being is like gold or silver or stone — an image made by man's design and skill. 30In the past God overlooked such ignorance, but now he commands all people everywhere to repent. 31For he has set a day when he will judge the world with justice by the man he has appointed. He has given proof of this to all men by raising him from the dead."

32When they heard about the resurrection of the dead, some of them sneered, but others said, "We want to hear you again on this subject." 33At that, Paul left the Council. 34A few men became followers of Paul and believed. Among them was Dionysius, a member of the Areopagus, also a woman named Damaris, and a number of others.

Why do you think Paul quoted the Greek poets that the philosophers were familiar with (see 17:28)? How can you use this idea as you share the gospel with others?

Read Acts 13:16-41. How is Paul's speech in Athens (see 17:16-34) different from what Paul said to the Jews (see 13:16-41)? How can you use this idea as you share the gospel with others?

NOTES AND OBSERVATIONS:

MEMORY VERSE

God's Remedy: The Cross

"Christ died for sins once for all, the righteous for the unrighteous, to bring you to God. He was put to death in the body but made alive by the Spirit."

— 1 PETER 3:18

The Acropolis in Greece:
Where Paul preached in Acts 17.

The Caryatids, also on Acropolis Mountain.

ASSIGNMENT FOR SESSION 4

1. **Scripture Memory:** Review steps 1 through 4 of "The Bridge to Life" (see appendix A) and memorize the verse titled "Humanity's Response" (John 5:24). Be ready to recite it during your next group meeting.
2. **Bible Study:** Complete "Session 4: Taking Stock of Your Spiritual Resources."
3. **Faith Step:** Using the four worldview questions from the upcoming chart, interview someone who holds a different worldview from you. Record his or her responses in the appropriate spot. If asked why you're doing this, simply reply that the assignment this week for a course you're taking has to do with understanding people in your culture. (You might want to use a photocopy of the chart during the interview and then transfer the information to this workbook page later.)

Name of Individual	
Worldview Represented	
QUESTIONS	RESPONSE
Where are we? What kind of world do we live in?	
Who are we? What does it mean to be human?	
What's wrong? What's the funda-mental problem with the world?	
What's the remedy? What will fix the problem?	

TAKING STOCK OF YOUR SPIRITUAL RESOURCES

ROAD MAP FOR SESSION 4

1. Pray.
2. Break into pairs and recite the memory verse titled "Humanity's Response" (John 5:24). Check off the appropriate box on your progress report if you recite it correctly.
3. Review each other's Bible study material and check off the appropriate box on the progress report if complete.
4. Share your experience of interviewing someone with a different worldview.
5. As a group, watch the video segment for this session.
6. With your group, work through "Session 4: Taking Stock of Your Spiritual Resources." Draw the video material into your discussion when it's relevant.
7. Pray.

SESSION OBJECTIVES

1. To identify the resources God gives us to reach the people around us who don't know him.

2. To understand more about the resources God gives us.

3. To gain a greater sense of confidence in the power of the resources God gives us.

4. To understand the relationship between Christians and the resources God gives us.

MY EARLY EFFORT

I'd been a Christian for less than a year. I lived on a floor of roughly fifty guys in a university residence. I really wanted to share the message of Jesus, so I invited them to a presentation of "The Bridge to Life."

I ordered a big tub of ice cream with all the toppings to make it more sociable. Six guys showed up, and we made enormous sundaes. Then I presented "The Bridge" on my dorm wall using a piece of cardboard and a black marker.

When I finished, the guys who came thanked me politely and then filed out of my room and went back to their studies. Needing some confirmation that all went well, I headed down to ask Cliff, a popular and intelligent exchange student from Wales, what he thought of the presentation. I noticed that the door to his room was open slightly, which meant "permission to enter" in the world of student housing. As I slowly edged open the door, I saw Cliff lying on his bed weeping, asking God to forgive him. Cliff had submitted his life to Christ!

As we talked, I discovered that it wasn't just my crude presentation that God used to bring Cliff to himself; God had mobilized many resources in Cliff's life to bring him to this point of surrender. His closest friends on campus were Christians who had been sharing with and praying for him. It was also clear the Holy Spirit was at work in him bringing conviction of sin and helping him see Jesus as Lord.

This was an important lesson for me as I realized that not only is coming to faith a process but God mobilizes many resources in a person's life.

In the same way a farmer knows how to use the tools of his trade, Christians should be familiar with the resources God gives us to share the message of the gospel with the people around us. This section will look at four essential resources that God gives us to accomplish this awesome task: the Holy Spirit, the Word of God, prayer, and the body of Christ.

RESOURCE 1 — THE HOLY SPIRIT

DAY ONE

Have you ever noticed a nice house or a well-designed building lit at night? When lighting is done well, the floodlights are so placed that you don't see them. Rather than seeing where the light is coming from, you simply see the building the floodlights shine on. This makes the building visible when otherwise it couldn't be seen in the darkness.

This image perfectly illustrates the Holy Spirit's role in our lives. He's like a hidden floodlight shining on the Savior. In essence, the Spirit stands behind us and throws light over our shoulders onto Jesus, who stands facing us. The Spirit's message is never "Look at Me; listen to Me; come to Me; get to know Me." Instead, the Holy Spirit is always saying about Jesus, "Look at him, and see his glory; listen to him, and hear his Word; go to him, and have life; get to know him, and taste his gift of joy and peace."[1]

THE HOLY SPIRIT AND THE WORLD

John 16 is the one place in Scripture where we see the Holy Spirit perform a work in "the world." The many other references to the Holy Spirit speak of what he *will* do in the lives of believers. This is an important passage because here "we see that the Spirit is not the domesticated auxiliary of the Church; he is the powerful advocate who goes before the Church to bring the world under conviction."[2]

KEY INSIGHTS	JOHN 16:7-15	GUIDING QUESTIONS
"THE COUNSELOR" (JOHN 16:7) This word is literally translated "called to one's side." . . . It was used in a court of justice to denote a legal assistant, counsel for the defence, an advocate.[3]	[7]"I tell you the truth: It is for your good that I am going away. Unless I go away, the Counselor will not come to you; but if I go, I will send him to you. [8]When he comes, he will convict the world of guilt in regard to sin and righteousness and judgment: [9]in regard to sin, because men do not believe in me; [10]in regard to righteousness, because I am going to the Father, where you can see me no longer; [11]and in regard to judgment, because the prince of	What sin does the Holy Spirit convict a person of? Whose righteousness does the Holy Spirit prove? How is this righteousness proven? (John 16:10)

	this world now stands condemned. ¹²"I have much more to say to you, more than you can now bear. ¹³But when he, the Spirit of truth, comes, he will guide you into all truth. ¹⁴He will not speak on his own; he will speak only what he hears, and he will tell you what is yet to come. He will bring glory to me by taking from what is mine and making it known to you. ¹⁵All that belongs to the Father is mine. That is why I said the Spirit will take from what is mine and make it known to you."	Whose judgment does the Holy Spirit convict a person of? How do you think this passage can help you when sharing your faith?
NOTES AND OBSERVATIONS:		

THE HOLY SPIRIT AND SHARING THE GOSPEL

In 1 Corinthians 2, Paul concludes his argument about the futility of human wisdom compared to the power and wisdom of God. The apostle accomplishes this by highlighting his effective ministry among the Christians in Corinth in spite of his weakness.

KEY INSIGHTS	1 CORINTHIANS 2:1-5	GUIDING QUESTIONS
"POWER" (1 CORINTHIANS 2:4) Denotes inherent ability, capability, and ability to perform anything; power to carry something into effect.[4] **"DEMONSTRATION OF THE SPIRIT'S POWER"** **(1 CORINTHIANS 2:4)** It were better to speak six words in the power of the Holy Ghost than to preach seventy years of sermons without the Spirit.[5]	¹When I came to you, brothers, I did not come with eloquence or superior wisdom as I proclaimed to you the testimony about God. ²For I resolved to know nothing while I was with you except Jesus Christ and him crucified. ³I came to you in weakness and fear, and with much trembling. ⁴My message and my preaching were not with wise and persuasive words, but with a demonstration of the Spirit's power, ⁵so that your faith might not rest on men's wisdom, but on God's power.	In the upcoming chart, list what Paul says he needs and doesn't need in order to deliver his message about Christ. What do you think it means to rely on a "demonstration of the Spirit's power" when sharing the gospel message?

NEEDED	NOT NEEDED

NOTES AND OBSERVATIONS:

DAY TWO

RESOURCE 2 — THE WORD OF GOD

Before engaging in battle, ancient soldiers spent considerable time training in the art of war. They often wielded swords, which could be used skillfully in battle as both offensive and defensive weapons.

God equips you with a tremendous instrument for spiritual battle: "the sword of the Spirit, which is the word of God" (Ephesians 6:17). The Holy Spirit uses the Word of God to accomplish the work of God.[6] As Christians, we need to saturate ourselves in the Word of God if we want to be used mightily on the spiritual battlefield. When we understand the source, ability, and power of God's Word, we'll see the importance of investing time getting the Word into our hearts.

THE SOURCE AND SUFFICIENCY OF SCRIPTURE

If we believe that the Bible is merely another book written by men, we won't have much confidence in it as a spiritual weapon. But if we believe we're handling the very Word of God, we can easily put our confidence in Scripture as a life-changing power. In 2 Timothy 3:16-17, we find an excellent summary of the way Scripture is both inspired by God and sufficient for our needs.

KEY INSIGHTS	2 TIMOTHY 3:16-17	GUIDING QUESTIONS
"GOD-BREATHED" (2 TIMOTHY 3:16) Inspiration is not dictation. Instead [God] put his Word into human minds and human mouths in such a way that the thoughts they conceived and the words they spoke were simultaneously and completely theirs as well as his. Inspiration was not in any way incompatible with their historical researches or the free use of their minds. It is essential, therefore, if we are to be true to the Bible's own account of itself, to affirm its human as well as its divine authorship.[7]	[16]All Scripture is God-breathed and is useful for teaching, rebuking, correcting and training in righteousness, [17]so that the man of God may be thoroughly equipped for every good work.	What or who is the source of Scripture? What four ways is Scripture of value to us? 1. 2. 3. 4. What's the end result of Scripture?

NOTES AND OBSERVATIONS:

THE POWER OF SCRIPTURE

Beyond knowing the source and sufficient nature of God's Word, we also need to understand the power of his Word. Hebrews 4:12-13 provides an excellent summary of how God's Word is powerful.

KEY INSIGHTS	HEBREWS 4:12-13	GUIDING QUESTIONS
"ACTIVE" (HEBREWS 4:12) Literally "in work." The Greek word is *energes* (or *energy* in English). The author of Hebrews was saying that God's Word is working.	[12]The word of God is living and active. Sharper than any double-edged sword, it penetrates even to dividing soul and spirit, joints and marrow; it judges the thoughts and attitudes of the heart. [13]Nothing in all creation is hidden from God's sight. Everything is uncovered and laid bare before	What are the attributes of the Word of God?

	the eyes of him to whom we must give account.	Read Isaiah 55:9-11. How does this truth, if believed in faith, build conviction when sharing your faith?

NOTES AND OBSERVATIONS:

DAY THREE

RESOURCE 3 — PRAYER

God provides prayer, which allows us to communicate directly with him. Christ, the great High Priest and Mediator, allows all Christians to come "boldly to the throne of grace" (Hebrews 4:16, NKJV).

Prayer can take many forms of expression, including adoration and praise, thanksgiving, confession, intercession, and supplication. Each of these enables you to draw closer to God. Because you can have two-way communication with God, be careful not to neglect your time with him.[8]

THE MINISTRY OF THE DISCIPLES

Matthew 9:35-38 fills a dual role: It summarizes the ministry of Jesus in Matthew 5–9, and it introduces the parallel mission of the disciples in Matthew 10.

KEY INSIGHTS	MATTHEW 9:35-38	GUIDING QUESTIONS
"COMPASSION" (MATTHEW 9:36) Literally refers to a gut reaction.[9] **"HARASSED AND HELPLESS" (MATTHEW 9:36)** Literally "torn and thrown down."[10]	[35]Jesus went through all the towns and villages, teaching in their synagogues, preaching the good news of the kingdom and healing every disease and sickness. [36]When he saw the crowds, he had compassion on them, because they were harassed and helpless, like sheep without a shepherd. [37]Then he said to his disciples, "The harvest is plentiful but the workers are few. [38]Ask the Lord of the harvest,	After Jesus told his disciples to pray for laborers, he sent them out (see Matthew 10:1-10). Why do you think Jesus did this?

"WORKERS" (MATTHEW 9:37-38) Literally "one who does something for wages." It is used for farm laborers.[11]	therefore, to send out workers into his harvest field."	Do you see and feel for lost people as Jesus did? Do you have a compassionate "gut reaction"? Why or why not?

NOTES AND OBSERVATIONS:

Read the following sets of passages about prayer and then think of a short phrase or sentence that can serve as a title for each set. What do the passages teach about prayer as it relates to sharing your faith?

• 1 Kings 3:5-14; Matthew 7:7-11; John 14:13-14; 15:7

• Genesis 18; Exodus 32:9-14; Daniel 10; Amos 7:1-6; Acts 4:29-31

MEMORY VERSE

Humanity's Response

"I tell you the truth, whoever hears my word and believes him who sent me has eternal life and will not be condemned; he has crossed over from death to life."

— JOHN 5:24

• John 14:6; Hebrews 4:14-16

• Matthew 21:22; Mark 11:24; James 1:6

• Psalm 66:18; Proverbs 15:8,29; 1 Peter 3:7,12; 1 John 3:21-22

RESOURCE 4 — THE BODY OF CHRIST

DAY FOUR

If we truly have experienced God's radical love for us, it should change our relationships to God, fellow Christians, and the world. In Romans 1–11, Paul told about all that God has done for us. In Romans 12, the apostle explained what our relationships (with God, fellow Christians, and others around us in the world) should look like as a result of experiencing God's love for us.

KEY INSIGHTS	ROMANS 12:1-21	GUIDING QUESTIONS
"IN VIEW OF GOD'S MERCY" (ROMANS 12:1) All that Paul asks his readers to do in this passage is based upon what he has told them earlier in the letter that God has done for them. **"BE TRANSFORMED" (ROMANS 12:2)** In the Greek *metamorphoo* is to change into another form (meta, implying change, and morphe, meaning form). This is the same word that is used of a caterpillar transforming into a butterfly. The meaning is "to undergo a complete change which, under the power of God, will find expression in character and conduct."[12] **"GIFT" (ROMANS 12:6)** The word *gift* is here used to denote a special gift or endowment bestowed by God on a particular believer to be used in his service and the service of the Church and of men generally.[13] **"BURNING COALS ON HIS HEAD" (ROMANS 12:20)** Most modern commentators have therefore concluded that Paul views "coals of fire" as a metaphor for "the burning pangs of shame." Acting kindly toward our enemies is a means of leading them to be ashamed of their conduct toward us and, perhaps,	[1]I urge you, brothers, in view of God's mercy, to offer your bodies as living sacrifices, holy and pleasing to God — this is your spiritual act of worship. [2]Do not conform any longer to the pattern of this world, but be transformed by the renewing of your mind. Then you will be able to test and approve what God's will is — his good, pleasing and perfect will. [3]For by the grace given me I say to every one of you: Do not think of yourself more highly than you ought, but rather think of yourself with sober judgment, in accordance with the measure of faith God has given you. [4]Just as each of us has one body with many members, and these members do not all have the same function, [5]so in Christ we who are many form one body, and each member belongs to all the others. [6]We have different gifts, according to the grace given us. If a man's gift is prophesying, let him use it in proportion to his faith. [7]If it is serving, let him serve; if it is teaching, let him teach; [8]if it is encouraging, let him encourage; if it is contributing to the needs of others, let him give generously; if it is leadership, let him govern diligently; if it is showing mercy, let him do it cheerfully. [9]Love must be sincere. Hate what is evil; cling to what is good. [10]Be devoted to one another in brotherly love. Honor one another above yourselves. [11]Never be lacking in zeal, but keep your spiritual fervor, serving the Lord. [12]Be joyful in hope, patient in affliction, faithful in prayer. [13]Share with God's people who are in need. Practice hospitality.	Once we experience God's radical love and mercy for us, our relationships toward God, the church, and the world (the non-Christians around us) should change. List how you think each relationship should change. Toward God: Toward the church: Toward the world:

| to repent and turn to the Lord whose love we embody.[14] | [14]Bless those who persecute you; bless and do not curse. [15]Rejoice with those who rejoice; mourn with those who mourn. [16]Live in harmony with one another. Do not be proud, but be willing to associate with people of low position. Do not be conceited.

[17]Do not repay anyone evil for evil. Be careful to do what is right in the eyes of everybody. [18]If it is possible, as far as it depends on you, live at peace with everyone. [19]Do not take revenge, my friends, but leave room for God's wrath, for it is written: "It is mine to avenge; I will repay," says the Lord. [20]On the contrary: "If your enemy is hungry, feed him; if he is thirsty, give him something to drink. In doing this, you will heap burning coals on his head."

[21]Do not be overcome by evil, but overcome evil with good. | How do you think these changes relate to spreading the gospel message? |

NOTES AND OBSERVATIONS:

"No skill of ours is going to be able to lead an inquirer to Christ. That is the sovereign work of the Spirit Himself. We never know whether our frail attempts to make the truth and challenge of the gospel plain to a friend will be crowned with success or not. The marvelous thing is that we do not have to concern ourselves too much about it. Our call is to be faithful stewards of the treasure of the gospel, which has been given into our charge. The Spirit's task is to apply it."

— Michael Green, *Evangelism Through the Local Church*

ASSIGNMENT FOR SESSION 5

1. **Scripture Memory:** Review steps 1 through 5 of "The Bridge to Life" (see appendix A) and memorize the verses titled "Assurance of Salvation" (1 John 5:12-13). Be ready to recite them during your next group meeting.
2. **Bible Study:** Complete "Session 5: Making Christ Known in Your World."
3. **Faith Step:** Fast for one day and ask God who he would like you to begin praying for. As you seek his will, complete the Acts 29 Prayer Circle (see appendix C). Begin to pray for the people listed on your Prayer Circle.

MAKING CHRIST KNOWN IN YOUR WORLD

ROAD MAP FOR SESSION 5

1. Pray.
2. Break into pairs and recite the memory verses titled "Assurance of Salvation" (1 John 5:12-13). Check off the appropriate box on your progress report if you recite it correctly.
3. Share your reflections on how your time of fasting and completing the Acts 29 Prayer Circle went.
4. As a group, watch the video segment for this session.
5. With your group, work through "Session 5: Making Christ Known in Your World." Draw the video material into your discussion when it's relevant.
6. Pray.

SESSION OBJECTIVES

1. To see that most people come to Christ as a result of a personal relationship.

2. To see that it makes the most sense to share our faith within our relational networks.

3. To identify the people who aren't following Jesus in our relational networks.

4. To identify obstacles that hinder us from sharing our faith.

5. To consider how we can overcome these obstacles.

CLOSE TO HOME

After four years of college in another province, I returned to my hometown. I remember really looking forward to getting my own place. I didn't mind being around my mom and brother; I'd just grown to love my independence. So I was somewhat disappointed when God tapped me on the shoulder and said that he wanted me to move back into my mom's house. I wanted to share my faith with my family, but not at such close range!

The two years that followed were some of the toughest years of my life. I often dragged my brother out of bed by the ankles to get him out the door to school. Some lifestyle issues in my family members' lives didn't mesh well with my own lifestyle in Christ. However, within two years, my mom came to Christ and I saw signs that the fallow ground of my brother's heart was beginning to soften.

Being back home also meant reconnecting with other people I'd known before college. At one point, I received a phone call from the cousin of an old friend, Jimmy, who told me that Jimmy was contemplating suicide. Jimmy and I began to meet each week to drink coffee and read Scripture together. Within a year, he came to faith in Jesus, but he still had some serious lifestyle issues to work through.

For one, he was hooked on intravenous drugs. And before he could overcome this

habit, a neighbor called Children's Aid, which took four of his six children into custody. Devastated, Jimmy called me in tears. I remember hanging up the phone and crying out to God because I didn't think that Jimmy's young faith could handle such a turn of events.

Children's Aid had two criteria for Jimmy and his wife to get their children back: He had to get "clean," and they had to move out of the nearly uninhabitable house where they were living. God came through for them by helping out with a down payment and helping Jimmy through his drug problem. Within a few months, the kids were back home and Jimmy's wife and one of their sons had made personal commitments to Christ!

Through these experiences, I learned some valuable lessons about sharing the message of the gospel. I realized that the most natural people to share my faith with were those closest to me. Our relationships provided a foundation of trust and mutual respect that made sharing the gospel natural and effective.

ADVANCING THE GOSPEL[1]

In the beginning of the book of Acts, we find that the gospel advanced naturally among a prepared group of people. A prepared individual or group of people has some sort of religious heritage. They've been exposed to biblical teaching and communities. Acts identifies the crowds that gathered in Jerusalem as "God-fearing Jews from every nation under heaven" (2:5). These people had been through years of cultivation and sowing and were ready to respond quickly to the preaching of the gospel.

Later in Acts, we see that Jewish believers scattered through the surrounding regions shared their new faith with fellow Jews as well as with Jews who'd adopted the Greek language and customs (see 11:19). The gospel advanced geographically. Yet apart from a few exceptions, through Peter and Philip the spread of the message of Christ was still confined culturally to Jews.

The emergence of an "apostolic team" finally took the gospel beyond the cultural confines of Judaism to other nations. The word *apostle* means "one sent forth." The word is used to describe the twelve disciples chosen by Jesus to carry the gospel to the Gentiles.[2] The task of the apostle was to plant and establish churches in areas where the gospel had not been before and where the people weren't "prepared." Unlike the Jews gathered in Jerusalem—or even those spread throughout surrounding regions who knew the Jewish Scriptures—these unprepared people had no religious heritage, so they didn't consider the message of Christ credible.

The question relevant to this session is, "After the apostles left town, how did the gospel continue to advance?" The quick answer is that local believers had to carry on by taking the gospel message into new places. The apostolic team had established a beachhead—a foundational generation. This generation had inside access to families, neighborhoods, places of work, and social networks. The believers in this generation were insiders. They were the key to the ongoing movement of the gospel.

DAY ONE

SHARING THE GOSPEL WITH PEOPLE YOU KNOW

Contemporary anthropologists generally agree that three social groups are culturally universal: (1) the family, (2) the local community, and (3) groups based upon common interests.[3]

Unfortunately, when people become followers of Jesus, they're encouraged, directly or indirectly, to abandon their relationships with people outside the Christian faith. However, when this happens, not only do the relationships suffer, it prevents the natural flow of the gospel through their lives.

God didn't intend for us to cut ourselves off from the people we know at the point we choose to follow him. We can see this by looking at how people in the New Testament shared their faith with those around them.

THE FIRST DISCIPLES: JOHN 1:35-51

In John 1, we see how five of the apostles came to encounter Jesus for the first time. Each came to Jesus in a different way.

KEY INSIGHTS	JOHN 1:35-51	GUIDING QUESTIONS
"THE FIRST THING ANDREW DID" **(JOHN 1:41)** Each time we meet Andrew in this gospel he is bringing someone to Jesus (6:8; 12:22), a consistency worth noting.[4] **"COME AND SEE" (JOHN 1:46)** Christianity did not grow because of miracle working in the marketplaces. . . . It grew because Christians constituted an intense community. . . . The primary means of its growth was through the united and motivated efforts of the growing numbers of Christian believers, who invited their friends, relatives and neighbors to share the "good news."[5]	[35]The next day John was there again with two of his disciples. [36]When he saw Jesus passing by, he said, "Look, the Lamb of God!" [37]When the two disciples heard him say this, they followed Jesus. [38]Turning around, Jesus saw them following and asked, "What do you want?" They said, "Rabbi" (which means Teacher), "where are you staying?" [39]"Come," he replied, "and you will see." So they went and saw where he was staying, and spent that day with him. It was about the tenth hour. [40]Andrew, Simon Peter's brother, was one of the two who heard what John had said and who had followed Jesus. [41]The first thing Andrew did was to find his brother Simon and tell him, "We have found the Messiah" (that is, the Christ). [42]And he brought him to Jesus. Jesus looked at him and said, "You are Simon son of John. You will be called Cephas" (which, when translated, is Peter). [43]The next day Jesus decided to leave for Galilee. Finding Philip, he said to him, "Follow me." [44]Philip, like Andrew and Peter, was from the town of Bethsaida. [45]Philip found Nathanael	In this passage, five different people have their first encounter with Jesus. Who are the five? Who introduces them to Jesus? What's the relationship between those being introduced to Jesus and those doing the introducing? Use the chart on page 66 to organize your findings.

and told him, "We have found the one Moses wrote about in the Law, and about whom the prophets also wrote — Jesus of Nazareth, the son of Joseph."

[46]"Nazareth! Can anything good come from there?" Nathanael asked.

"Come and see," said Philip.

[47]When Jesus saw Nathanael approaching, he said of him, "Here is a true Israelite, in whom there is nothing false."

[48]"How do you know me?" Nathanael asked.

Jesus answered, "I saw you while you were still under the fig tree before Philip called you."

[49]Then Nathanael declared, "Rabbi, you are the Son of God; you are the King of Israel."

[50]Jesus said, "You believe because I told you I saw you under the fig tree. You shall see greater things than that."

[51]He then added, "I tell you the truth, you shall see heaven open, and the angels of God ascending and descending on the Son of Man."

What do your findings tell you about one of the main ways the gospel travels? How can this apply to your life and your desire to share the message of the gospel?

	PERSON WHO MEETS JESUS	PERSON DOING THE INTRODUCING	RELATIONSHIP BETWEEN THE TWO PEOPLE
1.			
2.			
3.			
4.			
5.			

NOTES AND OBSERVATIONS:

USING YOUR HOME AS A MINISTRY CENTER

DAY TWO

Michael Green, senior research fellow at Oxford University, has explored just how the gospel spread in the early church. He wrote,

> *One of the most important methods of spreading the gospel in antiquity was by the use of homes. It had positive advantages: the comparatively small numbers involved made real interchange of views and informed discussion among the participants possible. . . . The sheer informality and relaxed atmosphere of the home, not to mention the hospitality which must have often gone with it, all helped to make this form of evangelism particularly successful.[6]*

In our times, many of us have very comfortable homes where we can invite the people we know to both hear the gospel message and see us live out our faith, even if we never "close the deal" by making a presentation. In Acts 10, we see how the apostle Peter entered a home and spoke to a group waiting there to hear him.

KEY INSIGHTS	ACTS 10:23-33	GUIDING QUESTIONS
"PETER" (ACTS 10:23) The range of the apostolic message had been steadily broadened. Already it had begun to cross the barrier that separated Jews from Gentiles; now the time had come for that barrier to be crossed authoritatively by an apostle. The apostle who crossed it was Peter, the leader of the Twelve, and the place where he crossed it was the largely Gentile city of Caesarea. The Gentiles who first heard the gospel from his lips were the family and friends of Cornelius, a centurion in the Roman army, belonging to one of the auxiliary cohorts stationed in Judea.[7] **"CAESAREA" (ACTS 10:24)** Caesarea, garrison port of Rome on the Palestinian coast, sixty-five miles from Jerusalem, was a foundation of the first Herod and a monu-	[23]The next day Peter started out with them, and some of the brothers from Joppa went along. [24]The following day he arrived in Caesarea. Cornelius was expecting them and had called together his relatives and close friends. [25]As Peter entered the house, Cornelius met him and fell at his feet in reverence. [26]But Peter made him get up. "Stand up," he said, "I am only a man myself." [27]Talking with him, Peter went inside and found a large gathering of people. [28]He said to them: "You are well aware that it is against our law for a Jew to associate with a Gentile or visit him. But God has shown me that I should not call any man impure or unclean. [29]So when I was sent for, I came without raising any objection. May I ask why you sent for me?" [30]Cornelius answered: "Four days ago I was in my house praying at this hour, at three in the afternoon. Suddenly a man in shining clothes stood before me [31]and said, 'Cornelius, God has heard your prayer and remembered your gifts to the poor. [32]Send to Joppa for Simon who is called Peter. He is a guest in the home of Simon the	What did Cornelius do when he heard that Peter was coming to visit his home? How can Cornelius serve as a model for us? How many members of your family don't know Jesus? What are some specific ways you can use your home as a way to tell your family members and others about the message

ment to that subtle diplomat's pro-Roman policy.[8]	tanner, who lives by the sea.' [33]So I sent for you immediately, and it was good of you to come. Now we are all here in the presence of God to listen to everything the Lord has commanded you to tell us."	of Christ?

NOTES AND OBSERVATIONS:

IDENTIFYING NON-CHRISTIANS IN YOUR SPHERE OF INFLUENCE

God created you as a unique individual, and he has placed you in a unique environment. You might be the only Christian representative to people within your sphere of influence. God has placed *you* there for a time such as this (see Acts 17:26-27).

If we want God to use us to bring people to him, we need to be involved in their lives in significant ways. Take a few moments to fill out the following chart, identifying non-Christian contacts you have in different spheres of your life.

SPHERE OF LIFE	NAMES OF NON-CHRISTIANS YOU HAVE CONTACT WITH	RELATIONSHIP TO YOU
Family (Parents, in-laws, siblings, cousins, aunts/ uncles, grandparents)	1. 2. 3. 4. 5.	
Local Community (Neighbors, coworkers, shop owners, mail carrier, school)	1. 2. 3. 4. 5.	
Shared Interests (Volunteer groups, athletics, unions, bridge clubs)	1. 2. 3. 4. 5.	

OVERCOMING OBSTACLES TO SHARING YOUR FAITH

When God asks us to respond to his call in faith, it's common to be afraid. The word *fear* comes from the Greek word *phobos*, which is where the English word *phobia* comes from. It can also carry the idea of running away or flight, caused when we're afraid.

FACING YOUR FEARS

DAY THREE

Fear is usually caused by the perceived or real intimidation of an adversary. Although it's one of the most uncomfortable and unpleasant emotions, fear isn't necessarily wrong. Our response to fear, rather than the absence of fear, is important.

Scripture addresses ways that, with God's help, we can move through our fears to a place of boldness and obedience in sharing the gospel!

KEY INSIGHTS	PSALM 34:4	GUIDING QUESTIONS
"FEARLESSLY MAKE KNOWN" (EPHESIANS 6:19) Responding to God in faith will confront us with frightening situations. As we lead in implementing our calling, God will take us into situations where we feel out of our depth and beyond the shores of safety and control. We will find ourselves in situations that only He can change. Any ministry based on vision and faith has to be this way. If it wasn't, why would we need faith? Our fears can work for us making us more dependent and drawing us closer to God, or they can paralyze and debilitate us. We will never run out of fears. There is always the smell of fear around the school of faith.[9]	[4]I sought the LORD, and he answered me; he delivered me from all my fears. **1 CORINTHIANS 2:1-5** [1]When I came to you, brothers, I did not come with eloquence or superior wisdom as I proclaimed to you the testimony about God. [2]For I resolved to know nothing while I was with you except Jesus Christ and him crucified. [3]I came to you in weakness and fear, and with much trembling. [4]My message and my preaching were not with wise and persuasive words, but with a demonstration of the Spirit's power, [5]so that your faith might not rest on men's wisdom, but on God's power. **EPHESIANS 6:19-20** [19]Pray also for me, that whenever I open my mouth, words may be given me so that I will fearlessly make known the mystery of the gospel, [20]for which I am an ambassador in chains. Pray that I may declare it fearlessly, as I should. **PHILIPPIANS 1:19-26** [19]I know that through your prayers and the help given by the Spirit of Jesus Christ, what has happened to me will turn out for my deliverance. [20]I eagerly expect and hope that I will in no way be ashamed, but will have sufficient courage so that	What specific fears do you have about sharing your faith with others? In what ways do your fears control your actions and limit what God wants to do through you when it comes to sharing your faith? What do these passages tell you about overcoming your fears?

	now as always Christ will be exalted in my body, whether by life or by death. ²¹For to me, to live is Christ and to die is gain. ²²If I am to go on living in the body, this will mean fruitful labor for me. Yet what shall I choose? I do not know! ²³I am torn between the two: I desire to depart and be with Christ, which is better by far; ²⁴but it is more necessary for you that I remain in the body. ²⁵Convinced of this, I know that I will remain, and I will continue with all of you for your progress and joy in the faith, ²⁶so that through my being with you again your joy in Christ Jesus will overflow on account of me.	What would it look like to share your faith boldly? How can you be bold and yet not lose your rapport with the people you talk to about the gospel?

NOTES AND OBSERVATIONS:

MAKING TIME TO SHARE YOUR FAITH

DAY FOUR

Time is valuable. But it's also easy to claim that we're just too busy to spend time with our friends and family members who don't know Christ.

Often this boils down to our priorities. As international preacher J. Oswald Sanders noted,

> It is often helpful to keep records of how each hour in a given week is spent, and then look at the record in the light of scriptural priorities. The results may be shocking. Often the record shows that we have much more time available for Christian service than we imagine.
>
> Suppose that we allot ourselves a generous eight hours a day for sleep (and few need more than that), three hours for meals and conversation, ten hours for work and travel on five days. Still we have thirty-five hours each week to fill. What happens to them? How are they invested? A person's entire contribution to the Kingdom of God may turn on how those hours are used. Certainly those hours determine whether life is commonplace or extraordinary.[10]

You can "create" time to spend with unbelieving friends by inviting them to join you in activities you already do. For example, if you like to go to the gym, why not go to the gym with a nonbelieving neighbor or friend? If you like to go to the movies, why not invite a nonbeliever to join you? If you want God to use you, you must recognize that you must give him time to do so.

Take a few moments to fill out this chart on your own.

Areas of my life in which I'm already involved with nonbelivers
Other areas of my life in which I could include nonbelievers
Areas of my life in which I can't include nonbelievers

Other times, internal obstacles limit our involvement with people who need to hear the gospel message. Which of the following issues keep you from being relationally connected with nonbelievers more than you already are? Check the ones that apply.

____ The offensive habits of unbelievers make me uncomfortable.

____ The unbelieving people I know don't have the same interests I have.

____ It's much easier to cultivate friendships with other believers.

____ I just never considered it "ministry."

____ I get affirmed as a person by my church involvement. With what I'm doing there, I have no time left.

____ I don't know any nonbelievers.

____ I'm afraid of getting drawn into their vices.

____ Other

ASSIGNMENT FOR SESSION 6

1. **Scripture Memory:** Congratulations! You've completed all the memory verses! Now memorize "The Bridge to Life" presentation on pages 141–143 and practice it on a blank piece of paper.
2. **Bible Study:** Complete "Session 6: Living Out the Gospel."
3. **Faith Step:** This week you'll complete two Faith Steps:
   - Continue to pray over and update your Acts 29 Prayer Circle as God leads. When a person listed on your Prayer Circle comes to faith, replace that individual with someone else God brings to mind. You'll keep praying for the person who has come to faith, just in a different way.
   - Identify where the people listed on your Acts 29 Prayer Circle sit on the process scale. The scale is provided again for you here.

MEMORY VERSES

Assurance of Salvation

"He who has the Son has life; he who does not have the Son of God does not have life. I write these things to you who believe in the name of the Son of God so that you may know that you have eternal life."

— 1 John 5:12-13

PHASE	CULTIVATION			SOWING			HARVESTING			MULTIPLICATION		
Metaphor	The Soil			The Seed			The Grain			New Crop		
Human Equivalent	The Heart			The Word of God			New Life in Christ			Spiritual Reproduction		
Application	Breaks up the fallow ground through relationship			Enacts the gospel through life, communicates the gospel through words, and embodies the gospel through community			Encourages a sincere decision to submit to Christ's lordship			New life begets new life in those within our sphere of influence		
Emphasis	Presence of believer or community of believers in the life of the individual, focusing on building bridges of trust and respect through relationship			Present the truth of the gospel by enacting it in your life, explaining it with your words, and embodying it in community			Persuade person to make a decision to submit to Christ's lordship			Reproduce new life in the lives of others; at this point, the process begins all over again		
Obstacles	Indifference Rebellion Ignorance			Ignorance Error			Love of darkness Indecision			Lack of training Isolation Lack of vision Self-centeredness		
Process Scale	-6	-5	-4	-3	-2	-1	1	2	3	4	5	6
Mini Steps Leading to Conversion	Indifference or hostility toward Christ	Aware of Christian's presence	Interested in Christ	Sees and hears message	Understands implications of message	Has positive attitude toward Christ	Recognizes personal need	Repents/believes/receives	New life in Christ	Is discipled in Christian life	Is equipped to minister	Reproduces spiritual life

Name of Person:

-6   -5   -4   -3   -2   -1   1   2   3   4   5   6

Name of Person:

-6   -5   -4   -3   -2   -1   1   2   3   4   5   6

Name of Person:

-6   -5   -4   -3   -2   -1   1   2   3   4   5   6

Name of Person:

-6   -5   -4   -3   -2   -1   1   2   3   4   5   6

Name of Person:

-6   -5   -4   -3   -2   -1   1   2   3   4   5   6

Name of Person:

-6   -5   -4   -3   -2   -1   1   2   3   4   5   6

ACTS 29

"You've had your chance. The non-Jewish outsiders are next on the list. And believe me, they're going to receive it with open arms!" Paul lived for two years in his rented home. He welcomed everyone who came to visit. He urgently pressed all matters of the kingdom of God. He explained everything about Jesus Christ. His door was always open.

STAGE 2

SOWING

LIVING OUT THE GOSPEL

ROAD MAP FOR SESSION 6

1. Pray.
2. Break into accountability partners and share your experience from the Faith Steps in session 5. Check off the appropriate box on your progress report if the exercises were completed.
3. Review each other's Bible study material and check off the appropriate box on the progress report if complete.
4. With your accountability partner, share the exercise of discerning where on the process chart the people listed on your Acts 29 Prayer Circle currently are. Spend some time praying for the people listed on each other's Prayer Circle.
5. As a group, watch the video segment for this session.
6. With your group, work through "Session 6: Living Out the Gospel." Draw the video material into your discussion when it's relevant.
7. Pray.

SESSION OBJECTIVES

1. To consider what it means for us to be the salt and light of the earth.

2. To understand that we've been called to be salt and light in our sphere of influence.

3. To consider why we've been called to be salt and light.

4. To consider how to be salt and light to the world.

MOTHS AND LIGHT

Shortly after my wife and I got married, we moved to a midsize farming town where she found a job teaching high school. I worked framing houses with a group of Christians and got involved with my local church.

Before long, I realized I was completely surrounded by Christians. I didn't have any contact with people who didn't know Christ, so I decided to join a flag football team in town. I ended up on a team made up of some pretty rough guys. One was a drug dealer, another was divorced, and they all liked to drink, swear, and fight. I realized that God has a sense of humor, as he placed me on a team of guys who were a lot like I was before I came to faith!

I really enjoyed the guys on my team, and a few of us began to hang out on a social basis. We'd go to movies, shoot some pool, and play football. It didn't take long for them to realize I didn't swear like they did. This made them feel uncomfortable—one of them even offered me five bucks if I'd swear just once.

Once they realized I was for real, they began to ask questions. Some of them even apologized when they swore in my presence, even though I didn't say or do anything to

make them feel guilty. One of the guys, Dave, began to have some deep conversations with me.

Six years later, I moved back to my hometown. Dave hasn't come to faith, but I know a seed was planted. And I still call Dave whenever I go to his part of the country.

This experience taught me that people who aren't following Christ notice a lot more about our lives than we think. God doesn't want us to judge them; instead, he wants us to live out a godly life before them. As nonbelievers watch our lives, they'll be like moths, attracted to the light of Christ shining through us.

THE CALL TO BE SALT AND LIGHT

DAY ONE

Jesus spoke about being both light and salt. In Matthew 5:13-16, for example, he issued a challenge to Israel to be the salt of the earth and the light of the world.

Salt served many purposes in biblical times. People used salt as a condiment to season food (see Job 6:6) and as a preservative to keep meat from rotting (see Exodus 30:35). Because of its medicinal values, newborn babies were bathed and rubbed in salt (see Ezekiel 16:4).[1] Salt was also used to season the Israelites' offerings (see Leviticus 2:13) because it symbolized permanence and incorruption (see Numbers 18:19; 2 Chronicles 13:5).[2] In Jesus' day, talking about salt indicated speaking about something important.

And light represents moral excellence. Jesus himself possesses this light, which gives soundness and character to all of life (see Matthew 6:22-23; Luke 11:34-36). Followers of Christ are also to be light because of the moral character they possess. Through believers, Christ sheds his light upon and reveals hidden defects in the lives of others (see Matthew 5:14-16; Luke 8:16; 11:34-36).[3]

Dig deeper into what Jesus said about salt and light in Matthew 5 and answer the Guiding Questions.

KEY INSIGHTS	MATTHEW 5:13-16	GUIDING QUESTIONS
"LOSES ITS SALTINESS" (MATTHEW 5:13) Rabbis commonly used salt as an image for wisdom (cf. Colossians 4:6), which may explain why the Greek word represented by "lost its taste" actually means "become foolish."[4]	[13]"You are the salt of the earth. But if the salt loses its saltiness, how can it be made salty again? It is no longer good for anything, except to be thrown out and trampled by men. [14]"You are the light of the world. A city on a hill cannot be hidden. [15]Neither do people light a lamp and put it under a bowl. Instead they put it on its stand, and it gives light to everyone in the house. [16]In the same way, let your light shine before men, that they may see your good deeds and praise your Father in heaven."	Summarize four functions of salt using a word or short phrase for each. 1. 2. 3. 4.

		What is the function of light?
		In what ways have you succeeded in being salt and light in your environment?
		In what ways have you failed?
		What steps can you take to bring more light and salt to the people you want to reach for Christ?

NOTES AND OBSERVATIONS:

The following passages help us understand why God's people have been called to be salt and light in the world. In your own words, write a summary statement for each passage.

Isaiah 49:6

Isaiah 60:1-3

Acts 13:47

| **DAY TWO** | HOW TO LIVE AS SALT AND LIGHT |

In Matthew 5, Jesus called us to be salt and light; the apostle Paul, in letters to various churches, then fleshed out how to do so. Let's look at several excerpts that deal with living as salt and light to the people around us.

KEY INSIGHTS	PHILIPPIANS 2:14-16	GUIDING QUESTIONS
"SHINE LIKE STARS" (PHILIPPIANS 2:15) The people of God are to "shine" in the world "over against" its darkness, while simultaneously they are to illumine that darkness. That is, by their attitudes and behavior they are to be clearly distinguishable from, and in opposition to, the world around them, while they are also to be God's messengers, bringing the word of life to the dying.[5] **"ANY UNWHOLESOME TALK"** (EPHESIANS 4:29) The word unwholesome (Greek: *sapros*) literally means "rotten, putrid, of a bad quality, refuse, depraved, vicious, foul, or impure."[6] **"THE WAY YOU ACT"** (COLOSSIANS 4:5) It remains true that the reputation of the gospel is bound up with the behavior of those who claim to have experienced its saving power. People who do not read the Bible for themselves or listen to the preaching of the word of God can see the lives of those who do and can form their judgment accordingly.[7]	[14]Do everything without complaining or arguing, [15]so that you may become blameless and pure, children of God without fault in a crooked and depraved generation, in which you shine like stars in the universe [16]as you hold out the word of life — in order that I may boast on the day of Christ that I did not run or labor for nothing. **EPHESIANS 4:29** [29]Do not let any unwholesome talk come out of your mouths, but only what is helpful for building others up according to their needs, that it may benefit those who listen. **COLOSSIANS 4:5-6** [5]Be wise in the way you act toward outsiders; make the most of every opportunity. [6]Let your conversation be always full of grace, seasoned with salt, so that you may know how to answer everyone. **1 THESSALONIANS 4:11-12** [11]Make it your ambition to lead a quiet life, to mind your own business and to work with your hands, just as we told you, [12]so that your daily life may win the respect of outsiders and so that you will not be dependent on anybody. **1 PETER 3:1-2** [1]Wives, in the same way be submissive to your husbands so that, if any of them do not believe the word, they may be won over without words by the behavior of their	In the left column of the chart on page 82, record the behaviors that each passage commands of Christians; in the center column, the impact of that behavior on nonbelievers; and in the right column, the Scripture reference. The first one is done as an example. What connection do you see between the way we live and the impact we have on those who haven't yet accepted Jesus as Savior?

"SEASONED WITH SALT" (COLOSSIANS 4:6)

Since salt prevents corruption, its presence would be a check on the "corrupt language" forbidden in Ephesians 4:29 — where the ministration of grace to the hearers is also enjoined.[8]

"TO LEAD A QUIET LIFE" (1 THESSALONIANS 4:11)

The verb rendered "to lead a quiet life" is used of silence after speech (Luke 14:4), cessation of argument (Acts 21:14), and rest from labor (Luke 23:56). It denotes tranquility of life, which of course does not mean inactivity.[9]

"WON OVER" (1 PETER 3:1)

The term "win" is a commercial term meaning "to get commercial gain" or "to win something," but in Christian usage it is a missionary term meaning "to make a Christian" and is used in parallel with "save" in 1 Corinthians 9:19-22.[10]

"PURITY" (1 PETER 3:2)

By purity the author does not mean simply sexual purity (as in 2 Corinthians 11:2), but the fully Christian character of the woman's life, especially her good behavior toward her husband.[11]

wives, [2]when they see the purity and reverence of your lives.

1 PETER 3:15-16

[15]In your hearts set apart Christ as Lord. Always be prepared to give an answer to everyone who asks you to give the reason for the hope that you have. But do this with gentleness and respect, [16]keeping a clear conscience, so that those who speak maliciously against your good behavior in Christ may be ashamed of their slander.

NOTES AND OBSERVATIONS:

A lighthouse is meant to be seen so that it can direct ships to where they need to go. In the same way, our good deeds should direct people's attention to God.

Christian Behavior	Impact on Nonbeliever	Passage
No unwholesome talk	Build up	Ephesians 4:29

Notes and observations:

DAY THREE

SALT AND LIGHT IN ACTION

We often think that our own society couldn't sink any lower. However, the apostle Paul dealt with societies in the first century that were at least as ungodly as our own. He wrote a letter to Titus, a young man he'd left in Crete to strengthen the church there. Cretans were known for their piracy on the seas, mercenary activity, homosexual religious rites,[12] and general depravity. Paul quoted the poet Epimenides, 600 BC, who said, "Cretans are always liars, evil brutes, lazy gluttons" (Titus 1:12).

Through this letter, Paul urged Titus to teach the Christians in Crete to live in such a way that their lives would sharply contrast with the rest of their society. The following passage provides instruction that outlines the characteristics of such a life — qualities that still apply directly to Christians today.

KEY INSIGHTS	TITUS 2:1-10	GUIDING QUESTIONS
"SOUND DOCTRINE" (TITUS 2:1) *Sound* comes from the Greek word *Hugiaino*, meaning "to be healthy, sound in health." This is where our English word *hygiene* comes from.[13] God is concerned with healthy teaching that results in healthy living. **"TEMPERATE" (TITUS 2:2)** Literally "sober." Signifies to be free from the influence of intoxicants.[14] **"BE SUBJECT" (TITUS 2:9)** The Greek word is *hupotasso* (*hupo*: "under"; *tasso*: "to arrange"). It was primarily a military term meaning "to rank under."[15]	[1]You must teach what is in accord with sound doctrine. [2]Teach the older men to be temperate, worthy of respect, self-controlled, and sound in faith, in love and in endurance. [3]Likewise, teach the older women to be reverent in the way they live, not to be slanderers or addicted to much wine, but to teach what is good. [4]Then they can train the younger women to love their husbands and children, [5]to be self-controlled and pure, to be busy at home, to be kind, and to be subject to their husbands, so that no one will malign the word of God. [6]Similarly, encourage the young men to be self-controlled. [7]In everything set them an example by doing what is good. In your teaching show integrity, seriousness [8]and soundness of speech that cannot be condemned, so that those who oppose you may be ashamed because they have nothing bad to say about us. [9]Teach slaves to be subject to their masters in everything, to try to please them, not to talk back to them, [10]and not to steal from them, but to show that they can be fully trusted, so that in every way they will make the teaching about God our Savior attractive.	Paul said that if we live according to Titus 2:1-10, we'll influence non-Christians around us in three ways. What are they (see verses 5, 8, and 10)? 1. 2. 3. What are the three negative ramifications if we don't live according to this passage? 1. 2. 3.

NOTES AND OBSERVATIONS:

THE CALL TO AN ETHICAL LIFESTYLE

DAY FOUR

The apostle Peter also discussed how Christians should live godly lives in order to be salt and light to the world.

Key Insights	1 Peter 2:11-17	Guiding Questions
"ALIENS AND STRANGERS" (1 Peter 2:11) The knowledge that they do not belong does not lead to withdrawal, but to their taking their standards of behavior, not from the culture in which they live, but from their "home" culture of heaven, so that their lives always fit the place they are headed to, rather than their temporary lodging in this world.[16]	[11]Dear friends, I urge you, as aliens and strangers in the world, to abstain from sinful desires, which war against your soul. [12]Live such good lives among the pagans that, though they accuse you of doing wrong, they may see your good deeds and glorify God on the day he visits us. [13]Submit yourselves for the Lord's sake to every authority instituted among men: whether to the king, as the supreme authority, [14]or to governors, who are sent by him to punish those who do wrong and to commend those who do right. [15]For it is God's will that by doing good you should silence the ignorant talk of foolish men. [16]Live as free men, but do not use your freedom as a cover-up for evil; live as servants of God. [17]Show proper respect to everyone: Love the brotherhood of believers, fear God, honor the king.	Underline every action in this passage related to being salt or light. List the influences that living the way Peter urges will have on people who don't know Christ as Savior.

NOTES AND OBSERVATIONS:

ASSIGNMENT FOR SESSION 7

1. **Scripture Memory:** Continue to memorize "The Bridge to Life." During next week's meeting, you and your accountability partner will practice "The Bridge to Life" with each other during the session.

2. **Bible Study:** Complete "Session 7: Embodying the Gospel Through Community."

3. **Faith Step:** Serve someone listed on your Acts 29 Prayer Circle. It could be something as simple as taking out a friend's garbage, actively listening to him share a problem, or shoveling his snow. Pray that God would use your good deed to demonstrate his love for that person. Be careful to not make the individual feel like a "project."

_____

_____

_____

_____

_____

_____

_____

_____

_____

_____

_____

"As salt we should season our world with the celebrant, confident, optimistic, and joyous nature of our position and privileges in Jesus. Because of all we have in Jesus, life is rich and free. By contrast, ultimately, life without Jesus is hollow, tasteless, and an empty pursuit. Our mission is to engage a world that has gone flat on itself with the zest and added value that Jesus brings to life."

— Joseph M. Stowell, *The Trouble with Jesus*

EMBODYING THE GOSPEL THROUGH COMMUNITY

ROAD MAP FOR SESSION 7

1. Pray.
2. Practice "The Bridge" with your accountability partner.
3. Review each other's Bible study material and check off the appropriate box on the progress report if complete.
4. Come back together as a group and share how your relational time went. Check off the appropriate Faith Step box on your progress report if completed.
5. As a group, watch the video segment for this session.
6. With your group, work through "Session 7: Embodying the Gospel Through Community." Draw the video material into your discussion when it's relevant.
7. Pray.

SESSION OBJECTIVES

1. To understand the purpose of Christian community.

2. To understand what a biblically functioning community looks like.

3. To consider how we can reach people with the gospel through authentic Christian community.

COMMUNITY DINNER

Each Thursday evening, the group of Christian university students I lead gathers for a meal and a time of teaching and discussion. People within this community take turns cooking for one another, and the general atmosphere is unhurried yet purposeful.

Sometimes people who don't know Jesus come to our meetings with a friend or somehow find their way to the gathering on their own. When these non-Christians come, they inevitably comment on how the people love one another and how they feel genuinely loved and accepted. I remember one student who wasn't a follower of Jesus declaring, "Everybody here really loves one another. I've never seen anything like this on campus before."

Once, during an end-of-the-year celebration we held, each person had an opportunity to share thoughts and feelings about the past year. One female student (who also wasn't a Christian) began to share how she loved our community. With tears running down her face, she told how much she'd miss our gatherings over the summer.

What's the result of such a community? Over the past few years, we've seen several people remain in our community and enter into a relationship with Jesus. Our

community served as an appetizer of what they could experience if they entered into God's kingdom community as a full participant.

DAY ONE

OVERVIEW OF BIBLICAL COMMUNITY

If you flew over a city, you'd see the general outline of the buildings, the layout of the streets, and some of the natural landscape. However, if you got into your car and drove through the same city, your perspective would be quite different. You'd be able to see the unique architecture of the buildings, the types of cars being driven, and the people who live there.

Reading the following Day 1 Bible passages is like flying over a city, as the passages provide an overview of authentic biblical community, showing the overarching purpose of community and a glimpse of what a functioning biblical community looks like. During Day 2 and Day 3 of your study, you'll "get in your car" and drive through these communities in order to get a more detailed picture.

Community is God's way of revealing himself to the world. Christians are to be like a showcase, on display for the world to see. When we live in authentic biblical community, the world catches a glimpse of what it's like to be a part of God's family. Perhaps even more important, others catch a glimpse of what God is like and what he's doing in the world. Without authentic biblical community and the love that characterizes it, it will be difficult to reach those outside the kingdom of God.

Consider the following passages from the life of the early church. Examine the purpose of these first Christians and how they interacted with one another.

KEY INSIGHTS	ACTS 2:42-47	GUIDING QUESTIONS
"FELLOWSHIP" (ACTS 2:42) *Koinonia*: communion, fellowship, sharing in common (from *koinos*, "common").[1] **"THEY SHARED EVERYTHING THEY HAD" (ACTS 4:32)** The word "shared" in this verse is *koina* (which is the same root word for fellowship found in Acts 2:42).	[42]They devoted themselves to the apostles' teaching and to the fellowship, to the breaking of bread and to prayer. [43]Everyone was filled with awe, and many wonders and miraculous signs were done by the apostles. [44]All the believers were together and had everything in common. [45]Selling their possessions and goods, they gave to anyone as he had need. [46]Every day they continued to meet together in the temple courts. They broke bread in their homes and ate together with glad and sincere hearts, [47]praising God and enjoying the favor of all the people. And the Lord added to their number daily those who were being saved. **ACTS 4:32-35** [32]All the believers were one in heart and mind. No one claimed that any of his possessions was his own, but they shared	According to Acts 2:42-47, what four things did this new community of believers devote themselves to? 1. 2. 3. 4.

everything they had. [33]With great power the apostles continued to testify to the resurrection of the Lord Jesus, and much grace was upon them all. [34]There were no needy persons among them. For from time to time those who owned lands or houses sold them, brought the money from the sales [35]and put it at the apostles' feet, and it was distributed to anyone as he had need.

ACTS 6:1-7

[1]In those days when the number of disciples was increasing, the Grecian Jews among them complained against the Hebraic Jews because their widows were being overlooked in the daily distribution of food. [2]So the Twelve gathered all the disciples together and said, "It would not be right for us to neglect the ministry of the word of God in order to wait on tables. [3]Brothers, choose seven men from among you who are known to be full of the Spirit and wisdom. We will turn this responsibility over to them [4]and will give our attention to prayer and the ministry of the word."

[5]This proposal pleased the whole group. They chose Stephen, a man full of faith and of the Holy Spirit; also Philip, Procorus, Nicanor, Timon, Parmenas, and Nicolas from Antioch, a convert to Judaism. [6]They presented these men to the apostles, who prayed and laid their hands on them. [7]So the word of God spread. The number of disciples in Jerusalem increased rapidly, and a large number of priests became obedient to the faith.

How did the life of Christ show through, both in the lives of individual members and the life of the community as a whole?

What can we learn from the study of the word *koinonia* (fellowship)? How does this facilitate our understanding of community?

How does authentic biblical community influence those outside the kingdom (see Acts 2:47; 4:33; 6:7)?

How does the Christian community in Acts 4 and 6 provide a skeptical world with a glimpse of what God is like? How could you apply this to your context today?

NOTES AND OBSERVATIONS:

DAYS TWO & THREE

A CLOSER LOOK AT COMMUNITY

When we live out the idea of biblical community in an authentic way, we draw in people who don't know Christ. The following passages provide us with an up close view of Christian community and help us understand how we should relate to one another.

KEY INSIGHTS	ROMANS 12:10-13	GUIDING QUESTIONS
"DEVOTED TO ONE ANOTHER IN BROTHERLY LOVE" (ROMANS 12:10) Christians [are] to be "devoted" (*philostorgoi*) to one another in "brotherly love" (*philadelphia*). Both key terms in this exhortation, which share the *philo* (love) stem, convey the sense of family relationships. Paul here reflects the early Christian understanding of the church as an extended family, whose members, bound together in intimate fellowship, should exhibit toward one another a heartfelt and consistent concern.[2] **"ONE ANOTHER" (1 CORINTHIANS 1:10)** The Epistles contain thirty-five "one another" commands that guide believers on how to live with each other in authentic Christian community. **"FREEDOM" (GALATIANS 5:13)** The phraseology is that of manumission from slavery, which among the Greeks was effected by a legal fiction, according to which the manumitted slave was purchased by a god; as the slave could not provide the money, the master paid it into the temple Treasury in the presence of the slave. . . . No one could enslave him again, as he was the property of the god.[3]	[10]Be devoted to one another in brotherly love. Honor one another above yourselves. [11]Never be lacking in zeal, but keep your spiritual fervor, serving the Lord. [12]Be joyful in hope, patient in affliction, faithful in prayer. [13]Share with God's people who are in need. Practice hospitality. **ROMANS 12:15-16** [15]Rejoice with those who rejoice; mourn with those who mourn. [16]Live in harmony with one another. Do not be proud, but be willing to associate with people of low position. Do not be conceited. **1 CORINTHIANS 1:10** [10]I appeal to you, brothers, in the name of our Lord Jesus Christ, that all of you agree with one another so that there may be no divisions among you and that you may be perfectly united in mind and thought. **1 CORINTHIANS 5:9-13** [9]I have written you in my letter not to associate with sexually immoral people — [10]not at all meaning the people of this world who are immoral, or the greedy and swindlers, or idolaters. In that case you would have to leave this world. [11]But now I am writing you that you must not associate with anyone who calls himself a brother but is sexually immoral or greedy, an idolater or a slanderer, a drunkard or a swindler. With such a man do not even eat. [12]What business is it of mine to judge those outside the church? Are you not to judge those inside? [13]God will judge those outside. "Expel the wicked man from among you."	As you read these passages, underline words that describe the way believers should relate to one another. In biblical times, community was expressed in the context of the households coming together. In the Greco-Roman world, households consisted of blood relatives, slaves, employees, clients, and friends. Using this broad definition of a household, how could you utilize your "household" to create community and reach out to those who don't know Christ? Place an asterisk beside those functions that can be carried out only through interdependent relationships. What does this tell us?

"LOVE EACH OTHER DEEPLY" (1 PETER 4:8)

The chief way in which we are to show ourselves children, not of the darkness of this present world, but of God's new day, is by loving one another — and that energetically and persistently, in the face of all discouragements. "[Deeply]" gives perhaps a wrong nuance; for it might suggest that the emphasis is on warmth of emotion, whereas the Greek word it represents . . . suggests rather the taut muscle of strenuous and sustained effort, as of an athlete.[4]

GALATIANS 5:13

13You, my brothers, were called to be free. But do not use your freedom to indulge the sinful nature; rather, serve one another in love.

GALATIANS 6:1

1Brothers, if someone is caught in a sin, you who are spiritual should restore him gently. But watch yourself, or you also may be tempted.

EPHESIANS 4:32

32Be kind and compassionate to one another, forgiving each other, just as in Christ God forgave you.

PHILIPPIANS 2:2-4

2Make my joy complete by being like-minded, having the same love, being one in spirit and purpose. 3Do nothing out of selfish ambition or vain conceit, but in humility consider others better than yourselves. 4Each of you should look not only to your own interests, but also to the interests of others.

1 THESSALONIANS 5:11

11Encourage one another and build each other up, just as in fact you are doing.

JAMES 2:15-16

15Suppose a brother or sister is without clothes and daily food. 16If one of you says to him, "Go, I wish you well; keep warm and well fed," but does nothing about his physical needs, what good is it?

1 PETER 4:8-11

8Above all, love each other deeply, because love covers over a multitude of sins. 9Offer hospitality to one another without grumbling. 10Each one should use whatever gift he has received to serve others, faithfully administering God's grace in its various forms. 11If anyone speaks, he should do it as one speaking the very words of God. If anyone serves, he should do it with the strength God provides, so that in all things God may be praised through Jesus Christ. To him be the glory and the power for ever and ever. Amen.

What gets in the way of interdependence?

The church is one very important form of community. What other forms could we use to build authentic biblical community?

How could these new forms of community be used to reach people with the gospel?

	1 John 3:16-17 [16]This is how we know what love is: Jesus Christ laid down his life for us. And we ought to lay down our lives for our brothers. [17]If anyone has material possessions and sees his brother in need but has no pity on him, how can the love of God be in him?	
	NOTES AND OBSERVATIONS:	

Understanding and living out authentic Christian community is important. God designed this community to function as one of the primary ways for the message of the gospel to reach the people around us. If we don't understand and live out community, we'll start to minister independently. However, that will limit what God can do through us, because we have less potential as individuals than we do as a team. A team offers more availability, giftedness, and resources.

THE COMMUNITY AND MISSION

DAY FOUR

Christian community is vital to advancing the gospel in our culture. In many churches, however, community and mission have become disconnected. Community is usually seen as the place where Christians meet for fellowship, Bible study, social events, and so on. But this shifts the purpose of the community from a group of people called to impact their culture to a group that exists only to build each other up.

When this distorted view of community exists, mission becomes something professionals do or that we do only during a specified time or event. As Mike Shamy, international vice president for The Navigators, puts it, "We are caught between conflicts of priorities. One is the care and equipping of the believing community. The other is the need of the surrounding unbelieving world. What takes priority—the ministry to the believers or the mission to the lost? Both, of course, are vital, but we have great difficulty keeping them together."[5]

The following Scripture passages can help you think about how your local church body can live out its mission of being an authentic biblical community.

KEY INSIGHTS	GALATIANS 6:9-10	GUIDING QUESTIONS

"TEACH . . . WITH SOUND DOCTRINE" (TITUS 2:1)

With the outside observer surely in view, it is precisely this behavior — of slaves, but also of younger men, younger women, older women, older men — in accordance with sound doctrine that it is able to project an accurate picture of life in relation to the God who saves.[6]

"A CHOSEN PEOPLE, A ROYAL PRIESTHOOD" (1 PETER 2:9)

In Old Testament times the role of the priest was to act as an intermediary between God and the people of Israel. From an international perspective, Israel was called to mediate between the Lord and all the nations of the earth (see Exodus 19:5-6). What Peter was saying is that the church now has this role to mediate between the nations and the Lord.

[9]Let us not become weary in doing good, for at the proper time we will reap a harvest if we do not give up. [10]Therefore, as we have opportunity, let us do good to all people, especially to those who belong to the family of believers.

TITUS 2:1-10

[1]You must teach what is in accord with sound doctrine. [2]Teach the older men to be temperate, worthy of respect, self-controlled, and sound in faith, in love and in endurance.

[3]Likewise, teach the older women to be reverent in the way they live, not to be slanderers or addicted to much wine, but to teach what is good. [4]Then they can train the younger women to love their husbands and children, [5]to be self-controlled and pure, to be busy at home, to be kind, and to be subject to their husbands, so that no one will malign the word of God.

[6]Similarly, encourage the young men to be self-controlled. [7]In everything set them an example by doing what is good. In your teaching show integrity, seriousness [8]and soundness of speech that cannot be condemned, so that those who oppose you may be ashamed because they have nothing bad to say about us.

[9]Teach slaves to be subject to their masters in everything, to try to please them, not to talk back to them, [10]and not to steal from them, but to show that they can be fully trusted, so that in every way they will make the teaching about God our Savior attractive.

1 PETER 2:9-17

[9]You are a chosen people, a royal priesthood, a holy nation, a people belonging to God, that you may declare the praises of him who called you out of darkness into his wonderful light. [10]Once you were not a people, but now you are the people of God; once you had not received mercy, but now you have received mercy.

According to these passages, what are some ways a biblical community can reach people with the gospel?

What do you think contributes to a community not reaching society with the gospel?

In Titus 2, Paul gave three reasons for the kind of behavior he was urging the Christians to exhibit: "so that no one will malign the word of God" (verse 5); "so that those who oppose you may be ashamed because they have nothing bad to say about us" (verse 8); and "so that in every way [Christians] will make the teaching about God our Savior attractive" (verse 10). What do these passages tell you about the purpose of this teaching?

¹¹Dear friends, I urge you, as aliens and strangers in the world, to abstain from sinful desires, which war against your soul. ¹²Live such good lives among the pagans that, though they accuse you of doing wrong, they may see your good deeds and glorify God on the day he visits us.

¹³Submit yourselves for the Lord's sake to every authority instituted among men: whether to the king, as the supreme authority, ¹⁴or to governors, who are sent by him to punish those who do wrong and to commend those who do right. ¹⁵For it is God's will that by doing good you should silence the ignorant talk of foolish men. ¹⁶Live as free men, but do not use your freedom as a cover-up for evil; live as servants of God. ¹⁷Show proper respect to everyone: Love the brotherhood of believers, fear God, honor the king.

How can your local church body live out its mission of being an authentic biblical community?

NOTES AND OBSERVATIONS:

"The family understood in this broad way, as consisting of blood relations, slaves, clients, and friends, was one of the bastions of Greco-Roman society. Christian missionaries made a deliberate point of gaining whatever households they could as lighthouses, so to speak, from which the gospel could illuminate the surrounding darkness."

— Michael Green, *Evangelism in the Early Church*

ASSIGNMENT FOR SESSION 8

1. **Scripture Memory:** Review steps 1 through 5 of "The Bridge to Life."

2. **Bible Study:** Complete "Session 8: Explaining the Gospel Through Words."

3. **Faith Step:** As a group, set up a social event before the end of this course. You might host a cookout, go bowling, go for a hike, or host a dessert night. The purpose of the event is to show how your group is an authentic Christian community. Each member of your group should invite one friend who isn't a follower of Jesus. The purpose of this time isn't to witness to your friends verbally but to let them experience Christian community and for you to enjoy them as one of God's beloved.

   Each person in the group should use his or her gifts to make the event as good as it can be (we touched upon gifting in session 4). If your gift is administration, you could organize the event. If your gift is hospitality, you could make people feel welcome as they arrive. In doing this, your team will be practicing an important biblical principle: teamwork!

_____

_____

_____

_____

_____

_____

_____

_____

_____

_____

EXPLAINING THE GOSPEL THROUGH WORDS

ROAD MAP FOR SESSION 8

1. Pray.
2. Break into pairs and practice "The Bridge to Life" with each other. Check off the appropriate box on your progress report if you get it correct.
3. Review each other's Bible study material and check off the appropriate box on the progress report if complete.
4. As a group, spend ten minutes discussing and planning your upcoming social event. Be sure to hold each other accountable for inviting an unsaved friend to this event. Check off the appropriate box if you've invited someone. (It's all right if the person you invited said no. The important thing is that you took some initiative. Perhaps next time he or she will say yes!)
5. As a group, watch the video segment for this session.
6. With your group, work through "Session 8: Explaining the Gospel Through Words." Draw the video material into your discussion when it's relevant.
7. Pray.

SESSION OBJECTIVES

1. To consider the necessity of verbalizing the gospel.

2. To consider the content of the gospel message.

3. To consider different ways to explain the gospel to others.

CONFIDENCE IN THE WORD

In the late 1990s, I went to New York City to take a course on sharing one's faith. Part of the course included going into different parts of the city, setting up an easel on the side of the road, and using it to paint an illustration of the gospel message and share it with whoever would listen. I was amazed at how many people would stop and gather around to listen. Throughout the week, I encountered many people who made professions of faith.

One of the participants at the course had turned his back on his faith for a while. He said he was walking down the street one day and someone handed him a pamphlet explaining the gospel. God used this tract to bring this man back to himself. Now he was taking a course on sharing his faith!

Another man worked repairing the sewers in New York City. One day, while down in

a manhole, he found a gospel tract that someone had thrown away. He cleaned it off, read it, and surrendered his life to Christ right in the sewer!

These experiences demonstrate a truth taught in Isaiah 55:10-11:

> *As the rain and the snow come down from heaven, and do not return to it without watering the earth and making it bud and flourish, so that it yields seed for the sower and bread for the eater, so is my word that goes out from my mouth: It will not return to me empty, but will accomplish what I desire and achieve the purpose for which I sent it.*

The main thrust of Isaiah 55 is about God's invitation of salvation. If we want to be effective communicators for the kingdom of God, we must have great confidence in his Word to bring people to himself.

THE NEED TO VERBALIZE THE GOSPEL

DAY ONE

In sessions 6 and 7, we looked at the importance of godly behavior and a loving community as foundational to sharing the gospel with the people we know. The third component of sowing is explaining the gospel using words.

Ideally, these three components work together. Unfortunately, we often want to separate words and behavior. Can't we just live a good life before others and let God take care of the rest? On the other hand, can't we just present a set of facts and not worry if our life matches our words?

Of course, the answer to both questions is that sharing the gospel is most effective when our words and actions work together.

When we think about verbalizing the good news, several questions come to mind:

- What message do I need to communicate?
- How do I talk to people about Jesus?
- How do I know the right time to initiate a spiritual conversation?

In Romans 10:11-17, the apostle Paul explained the extent of salvation—that God offers it to all people. Many Jews rejected the idea that God's grace extended to the Gentiles. However, from the beginning, Israel was meant to be a conduit of blessing to all nations (see Genesis 12:3). They were to be a kingdom of priests acting as an intermediary between God and the other nations of the world (see Exodus 19:6). Israel was to be a light that attracted other nations to God. However, the Israelites rejected this idea and became self-absorbed.

Most important, Paul explained the conditions that need to be present before a person can call on God's name.

KEY INSIGHTS	ROMANS 10:11-17	GUIDING QUESTIONS
"ANYONE WHO TRUSTS IN HIM WILL NEVER BE PUT TO SHAME" (ROMANS 10:11) This is a quotation from Isaiah 28:16. Paul's point is that salvation comes by faith (trust is the means) and it is universal in nature (the word *anyone* is used). **"GOOD NEWS" (ROMANS 10:15)** The Greek word for "good news" is *euangelizo*. It "is almost always used of the good news concerning the Son of God as proclaimed in the Gospel."[1] It means to make known "good or joyful news."[2]	[11]As the Scripture says, "Anyone who trusts in him will never be put to shame." [12]For there is no difference between Jew and Gentile — the same Lord is Lord of all and richly blesses all who call on him, [13]for, "Everyone who calls on the name of the Lord will be saved." [14]How, then, can they call on the one they have not believed in? And how can they believe in the one of whom they have not heard? And how can they hear without someone preaching to them? [15]And how can they preach unless they are sent? As it is written, "How beautiful are the feet of those who bring good news!" [16]But not all the Israelites accepted the good news. For Isaiah says, "Lord, who has believed our message?" [17]Consequently, faith comes from hearing the message, and the message is heard through the word of Christ.	Paul said, "Everyone who calls on the name of the Lord will be saved." What four conditions need to be met before someone can call upon the name of the Lord? 1. 2. 3. 4. If you just found out you'd won the lottery, how long would you be able to contain this information before you told someone? Do you feel the same way about the gospel? Why or why not?

NOTES AND OBSERVATIONS:

SERMON COMPARISON

Luke, the author of Acts, recorded three of the apostle Paul's missionary sermons: (1) the sermon preached in the synagogue in Antioch in Pisidia (13:16-41), (2) the sermon preached in Lystra (14:15-17), and (3) the sermon preached in Athens (17:22-31).

We looked at Paul's sermon in Athens in session 3, but by looking at it again along with the sermon he preached in Antioch, we can gain some invaluable insights about our own missionary activity. Read the following sermons and answer the questions in the chart on page 102. (You'll refer to this exercise for the rest of this week, so make sure you do a thorough job.)

PAUL'S SERMON IN ANTIOCH (ACTS 13:16-41)	PAUL'S SERMON IN ATHENS (ACTS 17:22-31)
[16]Standing up, Paul motioned with his hand and said: "Men of Israel and you Gentiles who worship God, listen to me! [17]The God of the people of Israel chose our fathers; he made the people prosper during their stay in Egypt, with mighty power he led them out of that country, [18]he endured their conduct for about forty years in the desert, [19]he overthrew seven nations in Canaan and gave their land to his people as their inheritance. [20]All this took about 450 years.

"After this, God gave them judges until the time of Samuel the prophet. [21]Then the people asked for a king, and he gave them Saul son of Kish, of the tribe of Benjamin, who ruled forty years. [22]After removing Saul, he made David their king. He testified concerning him: 'I have found David son of Jesse a man after my own heart; he will do everything I want him to do.'

[23]"From this man's descendants God has brought to Israel the Savior Jesus, as he promised. [24]Before the coming of Jesus, John preached repentance and baptism to all the people of Israel. [25]As John was completing his work, he said: 'Who do you think I am? I am not that one. No, but he is coming after me, whose sandals I am not worthy to untie.'

[26]"Brothers, children of Abraham, and you God-fearing Gentiles, it is to us that this message of salvation has been sent. [27]The people of Jerusalem and their rulers did not recognize Jesus, yet in condemning him they fulfilled the words of the prophets that are read every Sabbath. [28]Though they found no proper ground for a death sentence, they asked Pilate to have him executed. [29]When they had carried out all that was written | [22]Paul then stood up in the meeting of the Areopagus and said: "Men of Athens! I see that in every way you are very religious. [23]For as I walked around and looked carefully at your objects of worship, I even found an altar with this inscription: TO AN UNKNOWN GOD. Now what you worship as something unknown I am going to proclaim to you.

[24]"The God who made the world and everything in it is the Lord of heaven and earth and does not live in temples built by hands. [25]And he is not served by human hands, as if he needed anything, because he himself gives all men life and breath and everything else. [26]From one man he made every nation of men, that they should inhabit the whole earth; and he determined the times set for them and the exact places where they should live. [27]God did this so that men would seek him and perhaps reach out for him and find him, though he is not far from each one of us. [28]'For in him we live and move and have our being.' As some of your own poets have said, 'We are his offspring.'

[29]"Therefore since we are God's offspring, we should not think that the divine being is like gold or silver or stone — an image made by man's design and skill. [30]In the past God overlooked such ignorance, but now he commands all people everywhere to repent. [31]For he has set a day when he will judge the world with justice by the man he has appointed. He has given proof of this to all men by raising him from the dead." |

about him, they took him down from the tree and laid him in a tomb. [30]But God raised him from the dead, [31]and for many days he was seen by those who had traveled with him from Galilee to Jerusalem. They are now his witnesses to our people.

[32]"We tell you the good news: What God promised our fathers [33]he has fulfilled for us, their children, by raising up Jesus. As it is written in the second Psalm: 'You are my Son; today I have become your Father.' [34]The fact that God raised him from the dead, never to decay, is stated in these words: 'I will give you the holy and sure blessings promised to David.' [35]So it is stated elsewhere: 'You will not let your Holy One see decay.'

[36]"For when David had served God's purpose in his own generation, he fell asleep; he was buried with his fathers and his body decayed. [37]But the one whom God raised from the dead did not see decay.

[38]"Therefore, my brothers, I want you to know that through Jesus the forgiveness of sins is proclaimed to you. [39]Through him everyone who believes is justified from everything you could not be justified from by the law of Moses. [40]Take care that what the prophets have said does not happen to you: [41]'Look, you scoffers, wonder and perish, for I am going to do something in your days that you would never believe, even if someone told you.'"

	PROCLAMATION IN ANTIOCH	PROCLAMATION IN ATHENS
Who is the audience?		
What is Paul's starting point in his proclamation?		
What sources does Paul draw on to support his proclamation?		
From each of these sermons, what practical ideas about sharing the gospel can you apply to your life?		
What content is common to these proclamations? Go over the sermons and highlight the common points.		

WHAT TO PROCLAIM

DAY THREE

If you want to completely grasp the message of the gospel, a great exercise involves reading the book of Acts and noting the content of the gospel proclaimed by the apostles and others in the early church. Their approach, like that of Jesus, was never scripted. Their words contained deep theological truths, yet at the same time their message was deeply personal. They treated nonbelievers as individuals rooted in unique situations.

However, a basic framework or "pattern of sound teaching" (2 Timothy 1:13) provided a useful springboard for the memories of the early Christians sharing the gospel. This framework kept them on track. They turned again and again to pivotal points of the gospel. But this pattern wasn't a straitjacket that inhibited all imagination and initiative on their part.[3]

You might want to read through the book of Acts on your own, looking for the content of the gospel proclaimed by Christians in the early church. In this section of the workbook, we'll examine two key evangelistic sermons in the book of Acts. In the first, Peter preached to a group of God-fearers. A God-fearer is a person who believes in the

God of the Bible but has not entered into a personal relationship with him. In our context today, a God-fearer might be a person who comes from a Christian religious background but has never had a personal experience with the living Christ.

In the second, Paul and Barnabas preached to an exclusively Gentile audience. Gentiles were people who had very little knowledge of the God of the Bible. In our context, Gentiles are those who know little or nothing about God. They might be atheists, agnostics, or followers of other religions.

GOD-FEARERS HEAR THE GOOD NEWS: ACTS 10:34-43

As F. F. Bruce, who was a professor of biblical criticism at the University of Manchester in England, wrote,

> *The range of the apostolic message had been steadily broadened. Already it had begun to cross the barrier that separated Jews from Gentiles; now the time had come for that barrier to be crossed authoritatively by an apostle. The apostle who crossed it was Peter, the leader of the Twelve; the place where he crossed it was the largely Gentile city of Caesarea. The Gentiles who first heard the gospel from his lips were the family and friends of Cornelius, a centurion in the Roman army, belonging to one of the auxiliary cohorts stationed in Judea.[4]*

KEY INSIGHTS	ACTS 10:34-43	GUIDING QUESTIONS
"PETER BEGAN TO SPEAK" (ACTS 10:34) The scope of the *kerygma* (proclamation), as attested by this address of Peter's, is almost exactly the scope of Mark's gospel, beginning with John's baptismal ministry, and going on to tell of Jesus' ministry in Galilee, Judaea, and Jerusalem, of his crucifixion and resurrection, followed by the insistence on personal witness and on the coming judgment, with the offer of forgiveness through faith in him here and now.[5]	[34]Then Peter began to speak: "I now realize how true it is that God does not show favoritism [35]but accepts men from every nation who fear him and do what is right. [36]You know the message God sent to the people of Israel, telling the good news of peace through Jesus Christ, who is Lord of all. [37]You know what has happened throughout Judea, beginning in Galilee after the baptism that John preached — [38]how God anointed Jesus of Nazareth with the Holy Spirit and power, and how he went around doing good and healing all who were under the power of the devil, because God was with him. [39]"We are witnesses of everything he did in the country of the Jews and in Jerusalem. They killed him by hanging him on a tree, [40]but God raised him from the dead on the third day and caused him to be seen. [41]He was not seen by all the people, but by witnesses whom God had already	Highlight any words or phrases in Peter's sermon that his listeners needed to grasp if they were to have a proper understanding of Jesus. How does what you highlighted relate to you and anyone you explain the gospel to?

	chosen — by us who ate and drank with him after he rose from the dead. [42]He commanded us to preach to the people and to testify that he is the one whom God appointed as judge of the living and the dead. [43]All the prophets testify about him that everyone who believes in him receives forgiveness of sins through his name."	In what ways can this sermon serve as a model for explaining the gospel to people around you?

NOTES AND OBSERVATIONS:

GENTILES HEAR ABOUT THE LIVING GOD: ACTS 14:14-17

Acts 14:14-17 provides us with an example of what Paul and Barnabas preached to an exclusively Gentile audience.

KEY INSIGHTS	ACTS 14:14-17	GUIDING QUESTIONS
"GOD, WHO MADE HEAVEN AND EARTH" (ACTS 14:15) Preachers to such audiences would not be expected to insist on the fulfillment of Old Testament prophecy, as they did in addressing synagogue congregations; instead, an appeal to the natural revelation of God the creator is put in the forefront.[6]	[14]When the apostles Barnabas and Paul heard of this, they tore their clothes and rushed out into the crowd, shouting: [15]"Men, why are you doing this? We too are only men, human like you. We are bringing you good news, telling you to turn from these worthless things to the living God, who made heaven and earth and sea and everything in them. [16]In the past, he let all nations go their own way. [17]Yet he has not left himself without testimony: He has shown kindness by giving you rain from heaven and crops in their seasons; he provides you with plenty of food and fills your hearts with joy."	What did Paul and Barnabas explain to this audience that they didn't need to explain to Jews and God-fearers? Why did they explain this? Why didn't Paul get to finish his sermon? How is this passage relevant as you share the gospel with the non-Christians you know?

NOTES AND OBSERVATIONS:

METHODS OF EVANGELISM

DAY FOUR

As we've looked at the sermons in the book of Acts, we've identified the content of the gospel message. Now let's consider the ways the message can be delivered. After you read through the seven different methods of presenting the gospel, complete the exercise that follows.

1. Preaching

In Greek, several words are used for *preaching.* Two of the most common are:

- *Euangelizo* (where the English word *evangelism* originates). This word is used of the good news concerning the Son of God as proclaimed in the gospel. Examples of this word can be found in Acts 13:32, Romans 10:15, and Hebrews 4:2.[7]
- *Kerusso* means to be a herald or to proclaim. This word is used in Matthew 3:1 and Mark 1:45.[8]

2. Testimonial

The Greek word for *testimony* is *marturion* (where the English word *martyr* originates). A testimony contains truth from the gospel but has to do with the preacher's personal experience.[9]

3. Reasoning

The Greek word for *reasoning* is *dialogizomai* (where the English word *dialogue* originates). The word means "to bring together different lines of thought and weigh them."[10]

4. Teaching

The Greek word for *teaching* is *didasko*. It means "to give instruction."[11] Some people think that a person should be able to respond to the gospel message after hearing it once. However, learning is a process that takes time. J. I. Packer, professor of historic and systematic theology at Regent College in Vancouver, wrote,

> [The gospel] was a message of some complexity, needing to be learned before it could
> be lived by, and understood before it could be applied. It needed, therefore, to be

taught. Hence Paul, as a preacher of it, had to become a teacher. He saw this as part of his calling; he speaks of "the gospel: whereunto I am appointed a preacher . . . and a teacher" (2 Timothy 1:10-11, KJV). And he tells us that teaching was basic to his evangelistic practice: he speaks of "Christ . . . whom we preach . . . teaching every man in all wisdom" (Colossians 1:27-28, KJV, emphasis added). In both texts the reference to teaching is explanatory of the reference to preaching. In other words, it is by teaching that the gospel preacher fulfills his ministry.[12]

5. Hospitality

The Greek word for *hospitality* is *philoxenia*. It means "love of strangers," or "be not forgetful of." It's a compound word: *philos* (loving) and *xenos* (a stranger).[13]

6. Literary

Researcher Michael Green described the literary method as follows:

In addition to speaking to people about Christ, whether in public, in small house groups, or as individuals, one further method was open to the early carriers of the gospel. Those with the talent could write. And they did. In fact, they invented an entirely new literary form, the Gospel, to carry their evangelistic message.[14]

A vast wealth of solid Christian literature deals with issues and questions on most topics. If someone doesn't seem ready to go directly to the Bible, try to find out what issue he or she is struggling with and offer to find a book on that topic (see appendix D). Always ask the individual if you can get together to discuss the book at a later date. This keeps the dialogue going and provides opportunity to get that person into the Bible.

7. Personal

Michael Green also defined the personal method:

If public proclamation of various types and the private use of the home were crucial factors in the spread of the gospel, no less important was personal evangelism, as one individual shared his faith with another. The first chapter of John gives us the pattern. From the moment each man finds the truth about Jesus, he is constrained to pass it on. It was through the personal witness of John the Baptist that the two disciples found Jesus. No sooner had one of them, Andrew, made the discovery, than he found his brother Simon Peter and brought him to Jesus. Next, Jesus himself takes the initiative and encounters Philip of Bethsaida, we are not told how. But Philip carries on the good work and finds Nathanael, and he in his turn is brought to confess that Jesus is the Son of God. This is more than individualism of the author of the Gospel asserting itself. It is a reflection of the importance of personal evangelism in the outreach of the Church.[15]

Now that you've read the descriptions of the seven methods of sharing the gospel, complete this exercise by reading the following passages and identifying the method used.

In addition, think through and write down ways you can use that method to share the gospel with someone you know.

Matthew 28:19-20

Luke 1:1-4

> "For the word of God is living and active. Sharper than any double-edged sword, it penetrates even to dividing soul and spirit, joints and marrow; it judges the thoughts and attitudes of the heart. Nothing in all creation is hidden from God's sight. Everything is uncovered and laid bare before the eyes of him to whom we must give account."
>
> — Hebrews 4:12-13

Luke 24:45-48

John 1:35-51

John 4:39-42

Acts 17:16-17

Acts 28:28-31

ASSIGNMENT FOR SESSION 9

1. **Scripture Memory:** Review "The Bridge to Life."
2. **Bible Study:** Complete "Session 9: Preparing Your Personal Testimony."
3. **Faith Step:** Spend one day fasting and praying for those listed on your Acts 29 Prayer Circle.

PREPARING YOUR PERSONAL TESTIMONY

SESSION OBJECTIVES

1. To understand the importance of preparing our personal testimonies.

2. To learn how to prepare a personal testimony.

ROAD MAP FOR SESSION 9

1. Pray.
2. Share your experience of fasting and praying for those listed on your Acts 29 Prayer Circle.
3. Review each other's Bible study material and check off the appropriate box on the progress report if complete.
4. As a group, watch the video segment for this session.
5. Share your testimony with your accountability partner. Check off the appropriate box on your progress report after you've completed this. Provide feedback for each other.
6. Use some time to polish your testimony.
7. Break into groups of two or three and pray for those on each other's Acts 29 Prayer Circle.
8. Pray.

THE POWER OF STORY

Some years ago, I watched a film titled *Shadowlands*. The movie was a biography of the life of C. S. Lewis, an Irish writer and scholar.

In one scene, as Lewis sits in a bookstore doing a book signing, he spots one of his students stealing a book. Lewis follows the student back to his dormitory and confronts him. It turns out that the student has a voracious appetite for reading but doesn't have enough money to buy books. In the dialogue that follows, Lewis asks the boy why he likes to read. The student responds that his dad always said, "We read to know that we are not alone."[1]

Whenever I'm going through a rough time, I naturally turn to a story in the Bible similar to my own situation. As I read, I find comfort and encouragement knowing that someone has been through the same circumstances as I have and that a faithful and loving God always sees me through. The Bible contains many testimonies of God's grace and love for people who are hurting and broken, just like you and me.

Story is such a powerful medium for sharing the gospel message. As you share your testimony with others, you share the truth of the gospel while also sharing the difference that Jesus makes in your own life. When you talk to someone who has lost hope, is suffering, or is addicted, you can share how you've been through equally difficult situations yet God has faithfully seen you through.

In session 8, we explored explaining the gospel through words. One of the best ways to do this is through your personal testimony. In this session, you'll learn how to write your own personal testimony. I don't know of any better tool for preparing a testimony than one found in The Navigators' 2:7 series, so I'm including it here.

On your own during the week, prepare your testimony using this session. Then the next time your small group meets, you'll have the opportunity to practice giving your testimony to your accountability partner. And you can help each other refine your testimonies further.

WHY PREPARE A PERSONAL TESTIMONY?[2]

Although you'll be writing out your testimony, the purpose isn't to memorize it and deliver it verbatim. The purpose is to help you put into words some of the important and interesting details of your conversion. The choice of the right words, the flow of your story, and knowing how to begin and how to end are all important.

As you begin, ask God for wisdom and insight into just how to share your story. Be open to suggestions from your accountability partner and others in your group. Your testimony is one way to "be prepared to give an answer to everyone who asks you to give the reason for the hope that you have."

Trust God and work hard. Give time, thought, and prayer to this important part of your training in discipleship.

PREPARING YOUR PERSONAL TESTIMONY

1. Primary Aim
The primary aim is for you to complete and present your personal salvation testimony from an outline on a three-by-five-inch card.

2. Number of Drafts
The amount of time and effort it will take each person to prepare a personal testimony may vary greatly. This has little to do with intelligence or spirituality. It has everything to do with the complexity of your story. Some testimonies are extremely difficult to communicate clearly. Some have to be condensed. Others need to be expanded. So there are many factors that influence how long it will take you to complete your written personal testimony.

3. Difficult but Rewarding
Some people find this work on the personal testimony the most difficult part of the course, and sometimes the most discouraging. On the other hand, others find it the most profitable and stimulating part of the course. Your attitude and how aggressively you do your work can make all the difference. Work hard! Pray for God's wisdom and guidance.

4. Salvation Testimony

Testimonies can be prepared on many subjects and tailored to various audiences. The testimony you will prepare during this course will:

- Be designed to give to a non-Christian
- Be best suited for sharing one-on-one or in a small group
- Serve primarily as a "door opener," not a "convincing tool"

Many people are not ready to be convinced they need Christ but can often be led to talk about the gospel after an inoffensive presentation of a personal testimony.

EFFECTIVE PERSONAL TESTIMONY PREPARATION

Outline for Personal Testimony

Paul's testimony in Acts 26 is a biblical model you can follow in writing your own personal testimony. Paul's format in Acts 26 is:

- Lead-In: Verses 2-3
- Before: Verses 4-11
- How: Verses 12-20
- After: Verses 21-23
- Close: Verses 24-29

Guidelines for Preparing the More Specific Content

1. Make it sound conversational. Avoid literary-sounding statements. Use informal language.
2. Share, don't preach. Say "I" and "me," not "you." This helps keep the testimony warm and personal.
3. Avoid religious words, phrases, and jargon.

Religious Words	Possible Substitutes
Believe/Accept Christ	Trusted or relied on Christ for my salvation
Sin	Disobedience, breaking God's laws, turned my back on God
Accepted Christ	Decided to turn my life over to God
Cleansed by the Blood	God forgave the wrongs I had done
Saved/Born Again	Became a real Christian
Christian	Follower of Jesus

4. Generalize so more people can identify with your story. Don't name specific churches, denominations, or groups. Avoid using dates and ages.

5. Include some humor and human interest. When a person smiles or laughs, it reduces tension. Humor is disarming and increases attention.

6. One or two word pictures increase interest. Don't just say, "Bill shared the gospel with me." You might briefly describe the setting so a person listening can visualize it.

7. Explain how Christ met or is meeting your deep inner needs, but do not communicate that all your struggles and problems ended at conversion.

8. Sound adult, not juvenile. Reflect an adult point of view even if you were converted at an early age.

9. Avoid dogmatic and mystical statements that skeptics can question, such as, "I prayed and God gave me a job" or "God said to me . . ."

10. Simplify — reduce "clutter." Mention a limited number of people and use only their first or last names. Combine information when you can.

> *Poor:* "Martha Smith, Nancy Van Buren, and her cousin Jane Matthews came by my office at Digital Binary Components Corporation."

> *Good:* "Martha and two other friends talked with me at work one day."

> *Good:* "After living in five states and attending six universities, I finally graduated and got an engineering job."

Developing the Before, How, and After Sections

Here are practical suggestions for developing the Before, How, and After sections of your personal testimony.

1. Before

Many people's actions spring out of their unsatisfied deep inner needs. What were one or two of your unsatisfied deep inner needs before you came to know Jesus Christ? Some examples of inner needs are:

____ lack of peace
____ desire to be in control
____ lack of significance
____ fear of death
____ loneliness
____ no real friends
____ something missing
____ lack of security
____ no motivation
____ no meaning to life
____ lack of purpose

Non-Christians may try to satisfy their deep inner needs through unsatisfactory solutions. In the past, what unsatisfactory solutions did you use to attempt to meet those deep inner needs? As you develop your testimony, list positive as well as negative solutions you may have tried. Some examples are:

___ marriage/family
___ sports/fitness
___ hobbies/entertainment
___ work
___ money
___ sex
___ drugs/alcohol
___ education
___ wrong friends

2. How

Describe the circumstances that caused you to consider Christ as the solution to your deep inner needs. Identify the events that led to your conversion. In some cases, this may have taken place over a period of time.

State specifically the steps you took to become a Christian. If there is a particular passage of Scripture that applies here, you may want to use it. Usually you will simply paraphrase it.

Include the gospel clearly and briefly. The gospel includes:

1. All have sinned.
2. Sin's penalty.
3. Christ paid the penalty.
4. Must receive Christ.

3. After

State how Christ filled or is filling your deep inner needs. In the before, you expressed your needs and how you tried unsuccessfully to meet them. You now want to briefly show the difference that Christ has made in your life.

Conclude with a statement like, "But the greatest benefit is that I know for certain I have eternal life." The person you talk to will tend to comment on the last thing you say. Often it is natural to move from the testimony into a clear presentation of the gospel.

Two Ways You Might Organize Your Story

On page 114, you'll start considering which of three testimony formats you will use for your testimony. Here is some additional information that many have found helpful. Two possible ways to organize your story are to follow the chronological order or to use a quick overview/flashback at the beginning.

1. Chronological

With this approach, you tell your story in the chronological sequence in which it happened.

You might use this format if:

- You were converted later in life.
- You have enough interesting material to share prior to your conversion.
- Your conversion experience takes up most of your testimony because of the vitality and impact of the How. The Before would then be relatively short.

2. Overview/Flashback

With this approach you give an interesting, rapid overview of your life right up to the present. This overview takes the place of the Before in your testimony.

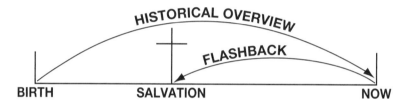

Then flash back to the spiritual dimension of your life. The flashback may go directly back to the How. This means that some Before might end up in your flashback. You might use this format if:

- You came to Christ at an early age
- You had an uneventful early life but have had a more interesting adult life
- Your How is very short

Choose Your Testimony Format — Samples/Worksheets

Read the three sample testimonies (pages 115–117) and then come back and decide which format best fits your own story. As you write the first draft of your testimony, refer to the sample testimony most like your own.

Format 1: Adult Conversion

You trusted Christ as an adult. You have a distinct Before, How, and After.

Format 2: Early Conversion/Adult Deeper Commitment

You need to evaluate whether the early conversion experience was genuine. If you conclude it was not genuine, use format 1 as your model. If it was genuine, your life has been characterized by spiritual immaturity or by a lifestyle similar to that of a non-Christian.

Format 3: Early Conversion/Consistent Growth

You probably grew up with Christian parents and have a strong church background. You may have very little Before.

Sample Testimony
Format 1: Adult Conversion
before

A few years ago, I found myself lacking purpose in my life. Something was missing. Nothing seemed to fill the void.

I had majored in electrical engineering in college and got a great job when I graduated. I kept striving for one promotion after another, thinking the next promotion would be the one that would satisfy me. But it never did. I began working longer and longer hours, giving myself to my profession. This began to have a negative effect on my family. I kept telling my wife that I was only doing it for her and the kids, but I knew otherwise. What started out as the "ideal" marriage was coming apart at the seams. It got to the point that I did not want to go home at night. "Happy hour" was more fun than arguments.

how

In my next job, I was asked to attend an engineering seminar with David and Jack from work. David seemed to have a certain something that was missing in my life.

On the way home from the seminar, David told me about how Christ had changed his life and had given him a whole new reason for living. Many of the things he said seemed to be directed right at me. He talked about having been successful in business but always falling short of his goals and expectations. Then he said that the answer to his frustration was personally committing his life to Jesus Christ. He had admitted to God that he was living in disobedience and had turned control of his life over to God. He mentioned that the Bible said Christ had died on the cross so we could be forgiven for everything we had ever done wrong. I had heard this before, but now it seemed to make a lot more sense. A couple of days after I returned home, I took a walk down by the lake near our house. I prayed and confessed to God some of the things I had done that I knew had hurt and displeased him. I asked Christ to come into my life and take over, as I wasn't doing a very good job with it by myself.

after

Well, there was no flash of light or earthquake, but I do know I felt as if a large weight was lifted from my shoulders. Not everything is perfect now, but I do feel I have a whole new purpose for living. God has given me a whole new set of priorities to live by. But the greatest thing of all is that I know for certain I have the gift of eternal life.

Sample Testimony
Format 2: Early Conversion/Adult Deeper Commitment
before

Not too long ago, you could have characterized my life as lacking any real inner peace. Everything around me seemed to be in utter turmoil. Nothing I did would ease the tension in my life.

It didn't seem as if anything could fill the longing that was growing in my heart. I thought I could fill that void by getting involved in activities. I joined the health spa, took tennis lessons, and was involved in transporting our children to all their various activities. I considered going back to work part-time. Then my husband received a promotion and we were transferred to another city. If I had felt the pressure before, the move just added to the intensity. It seemed the only relief I could gain was by taking tranquilizers, but that was only temporary and it scared me to realize I was beginning to depend upon them for relief.

how

We had gotten out of the habit of attending church over the years, but the Johnsons invited us to go to church with them, so we started going. After we had attended for a couple of months, we decided to participate in a Bible study discussion group. There we met people who were fun but took their Christianity seriously. They began to challenge us to really commit our lives to Christ.

We reviewed some things I had heard while growing up: that we were all breaking God's laws and deserved to be separated from him but that God had provided the way to restore that relationship with him; that provision was the death of his only Son, Jesus Christ. What I needed to do about it was acknowledge my disobedience to God and turn from it and ask Christ to come into my life as my Savior and Lord. So I asked Christ to take over my life.

after

It wasn't until we got involved in that midweek Bible study that I really understood what it meant to be committed to Jesus Christ. It was there that I learned I could not gain inner peace if I were going to try to run my own life. As a result of the Bible study, I made a whole new commitment to Christ. The inner peace I was striving for so desperately was finally there. But the greatest thing of all is that I know for certain I have a personal relationship with God and have eternal life.

Sample Testimony
Format 3: Early Conversion/Consistent Growth
before

As a single person, I see other singles feverishly trying to fill voids in their lives. They are into travel; some try the bar scene, dating, high-tech toys, sports, and even substance abuse. I also see married men and women (where I work) who are consumed with their jobs in extreme ways, often sacrificing their families in the process.

I'm involved in many of the same social activities as other singles. I love to play golf. I save up my money and take short trips overseas when the plane fares are low. But I have a contentment and peace that seems to elude many people. This new stability began in my life during high school.

how

As I was growing up, my parents were very active in church. Because they were active, they figured I should be also. So every Sunday, there we were. What was real to them was just a game to me. Then one summer, I attended a church summer camp. This changed my whole view of "religion." I discovered at this camp that Christianity was more than a religion; it was a personal relationship with God through his Son, Jesus Christ.

Some of the discussion groups centered around who Jesus Christ was and what he did. One day after sports, my counselor asked me if I had ever personally committed my life to Jesus Christ or if I were still thinking about it. I said I was still thinking about it. We reviewed some key Bible verses about what I needed to do in order to become a real Christian. From the Bible, I saw I had done things wrong and that the penalty was eternal death! I saw how Christ had died on the cross to set me free from that penalty. I said a prayer right there and committed my life to Jesus Christ.

after

As I grew physically and mentally, I also grew spiritually. I find that when I try to do things my way and leave God out of the picture, I have the same struggles as everyone else. But when I let him be in control, I experience a peace that can come only from him.

The stability I am experiencing through my relationship with God has impacted my job performance in positive ways and has helped me to be less self-centered. But the greatest thing of all is that I know for certain I have eternal life.

Testimony Worksheet
Format 1: Adult Conversion
What follows is a list of questions for an Adult Conversion testimony. Jot down thoughts under each question. This will give you a basis from which to write sentences and paragraphs about your own experience as you prepare your first draft.

before
1. What was a deep inner need in your life before you met Christ?

2. Give some examples of how you tried to meet or fulfill that need with unsatisfactory solutions.

"But there is no denying the zeal and the sense of discovery which marked the witness of the early Church in both their public and their private testimony, in both their written and their spoken word. It was this utter assurance of the Christians that they were right about God and Christ and salvation which in the end succeeded in convincing the pagan world that it was in error."

— Michael Green,
Evangelism in the Early Church

how

1. Describe the circumstances that caused you to consider Christ.

2. State how you trusted Christ. (Briefly include the gospel.)

after

1. Give an example of how Christ met or is currently meeting your deep inner needs.

2. End with a statement about knowing for certain that you have eternal life.

After you have filled in the Testimony Worksheet and are ready to start writing, you may not know how to begin. The following examples might trigger some ideas for you:

- A few years ago, I found myself lacking (deep inner need) in my life. (Develop the inner need.) I tried to meet that need by (develop the unsatisfactory solutions).
- A search for (deep inner need) would be the way you could have described my life not too long ago. (Develop the inner need.) I kept (develop the unsatisfactory solutions), but those things did not work.
- At one point in my life, I was searching for (deep inner need), but nothing I did would satisfy that need. I tried (develop the unsatisfactory solutions).
- Not too long ago, you could have characterized my life as/by (deep inner need). (Develop the inner need.) The things I tried did not help. (Develop the unsatisfactory solutions.)

Testimony Worksheet
Format 2: Early Conversion/Adult Deeper Commitment
What follows is a list of questions for an Early Conversion/Adult Deeper Commitment testimony. Jot down thoughts under each question to give you a basis from which to write sentences and paragraphs about your own experience as you prepare your first draft.

before

1. What was a deep inner need you were trying to fill?

2. Give some examples of how you tried to fill that inner need through unsatisfactory solutions.

how

1. Briefly describe the situation in which you made a deeper commitment in Christ.

2. Refer to your conversion experience. State how you trusted Christ. Briefly include the gospel.

after

1. State how Christ is currently meeting your deep inner needs.

2. End with a statement about how you know for certain you have eternal life.

After you have filled in the Testimony Worksheet and are ready to start writing, you might find it difficult to know how to begin. The following examples might trigger some ideas for you:

- A few years ago, I found myself lacking (deep inner need) in my life. (Develop the inner need.) I tried to meet that need by (develop the unsatisfactory solutions).

- A search for (deep inner need) would be the way you could have described my life not too long ago. (Develop the inner need.) I kept (develop the unsatisfactory solutions), but those things did not work.
- At one point in my life, I was searching for (deep inner need), but nothing I did would satisfy that need. I tried (develop the unsatisfactory solutions).
- Not too long ago, you could have characterized my life as/by (deep inner need). (Develop the inner need.) The things I tried did not help. (Develop the unsatisfactory solutions.)

Testimony Worksheet
Format 3: Early Conversion/Consistent Growth
What follows is a list of questions for an Early Conversion/Consistent Growth testimony. Jot down thoughts under each question. This will give you a basis from which to write sentences and paragraphs about your own experience as you prepare your first draft.

before
1. State the deep inner needs you see people trying to fill.

2. Describe how you see people trying to satisfy those needs.

how
1. Explain why this has been less of a problem for you.

2. Refer to your conversion experience. State how you trusted Christ. Briefly include the gospel.

after

1. Illustrate how Christ met or is meeting your deep inner needs.

2. End with a statement about how you know for certain you have eternal life.

After you have filled in the Testimony Worksheet and are ready to start writing, you might find it difficult to know how to begin. The following examples might trigger some ideas for you:

- As I look around me I see people lacking (deep inner need) in their lives. (Develop the deep inner need.) They try to fill that void or those needs by (develop unsatisfactory solutions).
- I feel that many people are searching for (deep inner need). (Develop deep inner need.) They try many things to meet their need, such as (develop unsatisfactory solutions).

ASSIGNMENT FOR SESSION 10

1. **Scripture Memory:** Review "The Bridge to Life."
2. **Bible Study:** Complete "Session 10: Bringing in the Harvest."
3. **Faith Step:** Before the next meeting of your group, share the gospel with a non-Christian friend listed on your Acts 29 Prayer Circle. You could do this by sharing your testimony, sharing "The Bridge to Life," inviting the friend to church, or lending a Christian book. Use one of the methods listed in session 8.

    Note: Pray for this opportunity. If God doesn't provide it, don't force it. However, if he does provide an opportunity, step out in faith and share. If you don't have an opportunity this week, ask God to provide one next week.

    To help you reflect on this time of sharing the gospel, fill in the following information:

    - Who you shared the gospel with

• Reflections on how the time went

_____

_____

_____

_____

_____

_____

_____

_____

_____

_____

_____

_____

_____

_____

_____

_____

_____

_____

ACTS 29

"You've had your chance. The non-Jewish outsiders are next on the list. And believe me, they're going to receive it with open arms!" Paul lived for two years in his rented house. He welcomed everyone who came to visit. He urgently preached all matters of the kingdom of God. He explained everything about Jesus Christ. His door was always open.

STAGE 3

HARVESTING

BRINGING IN THE HARVEST

COMING TO FAITH

Nearly two years passed from the time I began to seriously consider what the Bible had to say to the time I finally entered into a relationship with Jesus. I needed to come to grips with some intellectual issues first, such as, "How can I trust a book written thousands of years ago? Who was Jesus? Did Jesus really rise from the dead? Is Jesus really the only way to God?" My friend Ragnar—the Swedish guy who looks like a Viking—was patient and helped me work through these issues at my own pace. However, I still had some significant emotional barriers to work through.

I'll never forget standing with Ragnar in our kitchen in the university residence. He was trying to figure out what was keeping me from trusting Christ. I explained how my family had broken apart when I was ten and how I still felt such deep hurt and grief. Through my tears, I asked Ragnar the question that had been buried deep in my heart: "If God exists, then how could he let me experience so much pain?"

Ragnar also began to cry as he explained that although he didn't experience that kind of pain, he had witnessed a neighboring family go through a similar situation. I can't really explain it, but somehow that night I caught a glimpse of Jesus in Ragnar. I knew that God empathized and hurt right along with me.

Unlike some people who can name a date and even an exact time when they chose to follow Jesus, I can't pinpoint a precise time when I came to faith. But my salvation—my point of turning my life over to Christ and trusting in him—took place in and around this event with Rags. God broke through my barriers and began to bring healing and restoration into the parts of me that were wounded and broken.

WHAT IS CONVERSION?

DAY ONE

As we look at what salvation means, we can view it from two perspectives. When we see salvation from God's perspective, it's called regeneration. Regeneration is "a secret act of God in which he imparts new spiritual life to us. This is sometimes called 'being born again' (using language from John 3:3-8)."[1] When we view salvation from our perspective as humans, it's called conversion. As the people around us are born again by trusting in Christ as Savior, it's important for us to understand the dynamics of conversion if we want to be competent "midwives" during their "birth."

Wayne Grudem, professor of biblical and systematic theology at Trinity Evangelical Divinity School, wrote, "The word *conversion* itself means 'turning'—here it represents a spiritual turn, a turning *from* sin to Christ. The turning from sin is called *repentance*, and the turning to Christ is called *faith*."[2] In other words, faith and repentance are like two sides to the same coin. Both are necessary for conversion to take place. To gain a deeper understanding of conversion, let's examine each of these elements.

FAITH

In the New Testament, the Greek word for faith is *pistis*. This word conveys the idea of trust, reliance, assurance, and a personal surrender to God.[3] The Greek word for *believe* in the New Testament has the same root word as the word translated *faith*.

Our culture has weakened the meaning of the word *faith*, using it to describe an opinion that can't be supported by proof. Trust, reliance, and surrender are closer to the biblical idea of faith.

Faith has the following three components:

1. Intellect. In order to place your trust in Christ, you must know certain facts about Jesus' life, identity, death, and resurrection.
2. Emotion. Just knowing certain facts about Jesus isn't enough (see Romans 1:32; James 2:19). You can't just be aware of certain facts; you must also approve or agree with them.
3. Will. In addition to knowing and agreeing with the facts about Jesus, you must decide to trust or rely on Jesus to save you. When you make this decision, you move from being an informed observer of Jesus to beginning a personal relationship with him.

REPENTANCE

Repentance, as used in Scripture, can be defined as a "voluntary change in the mind of the sinner in which he turns from sin."[4] Repentance also has three components:

1. Intellect. In order to accept God's gift of salvation, you must recognize that sin involves "personal guilt, defilement, and helplessness."[5]
2. Emotion. Merely recognizing your guilt, defilement, and helplessness isn't enough. You also must feel sorrow and even hatred for sin.
3. Will. You can know you're guilty before God and feel sorrow about your sin. But you must also decide to renounce sin, forsake it, and lead a life of obedience to Christ. (Of course, this doesn't mean you'll never struggle with sin, but you'll desire and make the effort to obey Christ out of your love for him.)

We'll have all three components of both faith and repentance when we come to a genuine saving relationship with Jesus Christ. Here's how Augustus Strong, a well-known American minister and theologian who lived during the late nineteenth and early twentieth centuries, described the combination of these components:

The three constituents of faith may be illustrated from the thought, feeling, and action of a person who stands by a boat, upon a little island which the rising stream threatens to submerge. He first regards the boat from a purely intellectual point of view, it is merely an actually existing boat. As the stream rises, he looks at it, secondly, with some accession of emotion, his prospective danger awakens in him the conviction that it is a good boat for a time of need, though he is not yet ready to make use of it. But, thirdly, when he feels that the rushing tide must otherwise sweep him away, a volitional element is added, he gets into the boat, trusts himself to it, accepts it as his present, and only, means of safety. Only this last faith in the boat is faith that saves, although this last includes both the preceding. It is equally clear that the getting into the boat may actually save a man, while at the same time he may be full of fears that the boat will never bring him to shore. These fears may be removed by the boatman's word.[6]

In other words, we need to know certain facts that should influence our emotions and actions to the point that we throw ourselves upon Jesus because we realize that without him we are doomed. Let's look at some Scripture passages for illustrations of this.

THE PARABLE OF THE SOWER

DAY TWO

In session 2, we studied the parable of the sower as it relates to the process of evangelism. Let's look at the parable of the sower again as it pertains to conversion.

KEY INSIGHTS	MARK 4:1-8,13-20	GUIDING QUESTIONS
"[MULTIPLYING] THIRTY, SIXTY OR EVEN A HUNDRED TIMES" (MARK 4:20) Studies of the yield in Palestinian grain fields	[1]Again Jesus began to teach by the lake. The crowd that gathered around him was so large that he got into a boat and sat in it out on the lake, while all the people were along the shore at the water's edge.	In this parable, we find four different responses to the gospel. Below each one in the following list, identify the main element (for example, emotion, intellect, and/

where the ancient agricultural methods were followed show that a ten-fold harvest was a good yield and that the average was about seven and a half.[7]

"ALL BY ITSELF" (MARK 4:28)

This does not mean that the sower abandons his work, nor that he is uninterested in what takes place, for this is not the meaning of the reference to his sleeping and rising. It means that the seed must be allowed its appointed course; as the process of growth and ripening advances toward a harvest that is approaching. The sower takes account of the growth of the seed, but he cannot fully understand it. His ultimate interest is in the purpose for which the seed was sown — the harvest; when the grain is ripened, he immediately sends forth the sickle to the grain.[8]

"THE KINGDOM OF GOD" (MARK 4:26)

The stress in [this] parable thus falls upon the sowing of the seed as a messianic work which unleashes mysterious forces which operate of themselves in the achievement of the sovereign purposes of God.[9]

[2]He taught them many things by parables, and in his teaching said: [3]"Listen! A farmer went out to sow his seed. [4]As he was scattering the seed, some fell along the path, and the birds came and ate it up. [5]Some fell on rocky places, where it did not have much soil. It sprang up quickly, because the soil was shallow. [6]But when the sun came up, the plants were scorched, and they withered because they had no root. [7]Other seed fell among thorns, which grew up and choked the plants, so that they did not bear grain. [8]Still other seed fell on good soil. It came up, grew and produced a crop, multiplying thirty, sixty, or even a hundred times." . . .

[13]Then Jesus said to them, "Don't you understand this parable? How then will you understand any parable? [14]The farmer sows the word. [15]Some people are like seed along the path, where the word is sown. As soon as they hear it, Satan comes and takes away the word that was sown in them. [16]Others, like seed sown on rocky places, hear the word and at once receive it with joy. [17]But since they have no root, they last only a short time. When trouble or persecution comes because of the word, they quickly fall away. [18]Still others, like seed sown among thorns, hear the word; [19]but the worries of this life, the deceitfulness of wealth and the desires for other things come in and choke the word, making it unfruitful. [20]Others, like seed sown on good soil, hear the word, accept it, and produce a crop — thirty, sixty or even a hundred times what was sown."

MARK 4:26-29

[26]He also said, "This is what the kingdom of God is like. A man scatters seed on the ground. [27]Night and day, whether he sleeps or gets up, the seed sprouts and grows, though he does not know how. [28]All by itself the soil produces grain — first the stalk, then the head, then the full kernel in the head. [29]As soon as the grain is ripe, he puts the sickle to it, because the harvest has come."

or will) of faith/repentance that is the focal point of each response. Also, list what prevented or encouraged the growth of the seed.

1. The seed that fell beside the road

2. The seed that fell on rocky places

3. The seed that fell among thorns

4. The seed that fell on good soil

What do these parables teach us about God's role in bringing someone to faith?

What word would you use to describe the farmer in this parable?

How would you know when a person is "ripe for harvesting"?

NOTES AND OBSERVATIONS:

ENTERING A RELATIONSHIP WITH JESUS

DAY THREE

When Jesus invited people into a relationship with himself, he didn't always use words like *faith* and *repent*. Yet the terms he used conveyed the same message to those living in first-century Palestine.

KEY INSIGHTS	MATTHEW 11:28-30	GUIDING QUESTIONS
"COME TO ME. . . . TAKE MY YOKE" (MATTHEW 11:28-29) When Jesus invites sinners, "Come to me, all who labor and are heavy laden, and I will give you rest," he immediately adds, "Take my yoke upon you, and learn from me." . . . To come to him includes taking his yoke upon us, being subject to his direction and guidance, learning from him and being obedient to him. If we are unwilling to make such a commitment, then we have not truly placed our trust in him.[10] **"BELIEVED IN HIS NAME" (JOHN 1:12)** To believe, also to be persuaded of, and hence, to place confidence in, to trust, signifies, in this sense of the word, reliance upon, not mere credence.[11]	[28]"Come to me, all you who are weary and burdened, and I will give you rest. [29]Take my yoke upon you and learn from me, for I am gentle and humble in heart, and you will find rest for your souls. [30]For my yoke is easy and my burden is light." **JOHN 1:12** [12]To all who received him, to those who believed in his name, he gave the right to become children of God. **JOHN 3:16** [16]"God so loved the world that he gave his one and only Son, that whoever believes in him shall not perish but have eternal life." **JOHN 6:37** [37]"All that the Father gives me will come to me, and whoever comes to me I will never drive away." **JOHN 7:37** [37]On the last and greatest day of the Feast, Jesus stood and said in	Highlight or underline the words or phrases that Jesus uses when calling people into a relationship with himself. What stands out to you about these words or phrases?

"WHOEVER BELIEVES IN HIM" (JOHN 3:16)	a loud voice, "If anyone is thirsty, let him come to me and drink."	After reading the Key Insights, explain what conditions must be present for you to trust another person. What about a person trusting God?
Here John uses a surprising phrase when he does not simply say, "Whoever *believes him*" (that is, believes that what he says is true and able to be trusted), but rather, "*whoever believes in him*." The Greek phrase *pisteuo eis auton* could also be translated "believe into him" with the sense of trust or confidence that goes *into* and rests *in* Jesus as a person.[12]		

NOTES AND OBSERVATIONS:

YOUR ROLE IN CONVERSION

DAY FOUR

At some point, each person must make a decision—a personal response to the gospel. As we noted earlier, it's not enough to just understand and acknowledge the truth; each person needs to respond in faith and repentance.

Of the three elements (intellect, emotions, and will), the will usually holds out the longest against Christ. You might deal with all of someone's intellectual inquiries and emotional baggage, yet that person still holds out against Christ. What can you do at that point? Consider the following options:

1. The parables of the sower and growing seed clearly teach that conversion is God's work. Some people may never come to faith, others may take some time, and still others will come to faith rather quickly. The important thing to remember is that your role is limited. You need to be faithful in sowing seed and looking for Spirit-led opportunities to share.

2. The best way to lead someone into a relationship with Christ is to urge that person to read and discuss the Bible with you, and then pray. "Five Hours with John" (see appendix E) offers a good starting point as you get into the Bible with a spiritual seeker.

3. "The Bridge to Life" (see appendix A) is another excellent tool for helping people see where they are in the process. When you've finished presenting "The Bridge," you can ask people where they sit on the diagram. If they indicate the left-hand side of the bridge, ask them what's preventing them from crossing over to God's side. It might be a struggle with an intellectual or emotional issue. Once you identify the specific issue, you can offer to work through it with them. For example, if they're uncertain about the Bible's reliability, you can offer to loan them a book that deals with the issue and get together to discuss it.

Intellectual and emotional issues often serve as smoke screens. In other words, a person might say she hasn't resolved a particular issue, but when you offer to sort through it with her, she declines. At this point you might want to back off but continue praying for and loving the person. Perhaps God will bring about a change of heart or circumstances as time goes on.

However, at other times, an individual will acknowledge that nothing hinders him from "crossing over to God's side of the bridge." At that point, make sure he understands the implications of crossing over to God's side and ask if he'd like to cross over to God's side right now. If he does, pray with him and begin the discipling process as soon as possible (see session 11).

"We have the immense privilege, sometimes, of being midwives at birth. Every birth is special. Each one is a thing of surpassing wonder. And when you put it like that, it is easy to see two contrasting errors to which you could possibly fall prey. One would be to treat all births alike, with professional competence, but miss the individual needs and be blinded to the glory of it all. That way is sad and potentially disastrous, especially if there are any complications in the birth; and spiritually there usually are! The other mistake would be to be called upon to act the midwife and yet not have a clue what to do!"

— Michael Green, *Evangelism Through the Local Church*

ASSIGNMENT FOR SESSION 11

1. **Scripture Memory:** At this point, review the verses in "The Bridge to Life" a couple of times each week. This will keep them fresh in your mind.
2. **Bible Study:** Complete "Session 11: Discipling a New Believer."
3. **Faith Step:** Spend an hour of relational time with a person listed on your Acts 29 Prayer Circle.

ACTS

29

"You've had your chance. The non-Jewish outsiders are next on the list. And believe me, they're going to receive it with open arms!" Paul lived for two years in his rented home. He welcomed everyone who came to visit. He urgently presented all matters of the kingdom of God. He explained everything about Jesus Christ. His door was always open.

STAGE 4

MULTIPLYING

DISCIPLING A NEW BELIEVER

ROAD MAP FOR SESSION 11

1. Pray.
2. Share with the rest of the group how your one-hour relational time went with the person listed on your Acts 29 Prayer Circle.
3. Review each other's Bible study material and check off the appropriate box on the progress report if complete.
4. As a group, watch the video segment for this session.
5. With your group, work through "Session 11: Discipling a New Believer." Draw the video material into your discussion when it's relevant.
6. Pray.

SESSION OBJECTIVES

1. To understand what a disciple is.

2. To understand the basic components of the Christian life so we can help others grow in their newfound faith.

3. To understand that as Christians we've been called to make disciples not just converts!

THE CALL OF A PARENT

My wife and I had heard stories about how much work a new baby is. But stories don't prepare you for reality!

When Benjamin arrived, we were overjoyed by his presence. He was perfect, he was beautiful—and he was a lot of work. There were diapers to change, laundry to do, and bottles to warm. The amount of work was only compounded by the number of nights that we slept less than four hours.

But it has all been worth it. It's been almost five years since his birth, and those years of investing in Benjamin have paid off. He now has a degree of independence. He dresses himself, feeds himself, and even cleans his room sometimes.

Just as a newborn baby needs food, clothing, and general nurturing to survive, the people around us who come to Christ need us to come alongside them and provide for their needs until they're able to stand on their own. This process, called discipleship, is vitally important for the health and well-being of the church. Don't think of this as a job that God calls only church leaders to fulfill; he also calls *you* to be a spiritual parent.

If God has used you to bring a person to faith, there's a good possibility he also wants you to help facilitate spiritual growth in that individual's life.

WHAT IS A DISCIPLE?

The Greek word for *disciple* is *mathetes*, and it literally means "a learner" (from *manthano*, to learn). In the first century, a disciple wasn't just a pupil but an adherent—someone who becomes an imitator of the teacher (see John 8:31; 15:8).[1]

I can't think of a better tool to explain the basic components of the Christian life than "The Wheel Illustration." "The Wheel" is a valuable tool for gaining understanding about important spiritual disciplines in life. It provides a frame of reference for a discipling relationship. It helps us think clearly about what it means to be a well-balanced follower of Christ. I often use it in my discipleship relationships to help new believers grow in their faith. Other times I use it as a diagnostic tool in a believer's life. As we work through "The Wheel," it becomes apparent what areas a person needs help in and what areas the person is strong in.

Let's look at "The Wheel" step-by-step.[2]

This simple but effective illustration has been used by The Navigators for more than fifty years. It helps Christians understand what they are called to do as disciples of Christ. Each part of this illustration represents a crucially important component of a vital Christian life.

THE VOLITIONAL DIMENSION

How You Relate to Yourself
The Hub: Christ the Center
See 2 Corinthians 5:17; Galatians 2:20
Making Christ central in your life is an act of your will. Surrendering totally to Christ's authority and lordship may be at conversion or after some months or even years. God creates within you the desire to do what he wants you to do in order to express his lordship in your life.

The Rim: Obedience to Christ
See Romans 12:1; John 14:21
Some acts of obedience to God are internal. But even these internal acts of obedience—such as attitudes, habits, motives, sense of values, and day-to-day thoughts—eventually surface in relationships with other people. The proof of your love for God is your demonstrated obedience to him.

THE VERTICAL DIMENSION

How You Relate to God
The Word Spoke
See 2 Timothy 3:16; Joshua 1:8
As God speaks to you through the Scriptures, you can see his principles for life and ministry, learn how to obey, and become acquainted with the Christ who is worthy of your unqualified allegiance. A vital personal intake of God's Word is essential for health and growth.

To help your new-believing friend with taking in the Word of God, use "The Word Hand Illustration."[3]

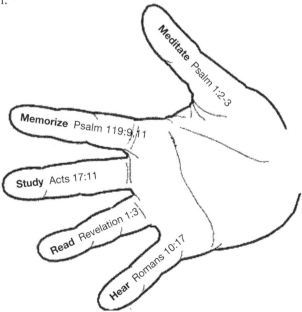

"The Word Hand" shows five very important methods of learning from the Bible.

HEARING

Romans 10:17

Hearing the Word from godly pastors and teachers provides insight into others' study of the Scriptures as well as stimulates your own appetite for the Word.

READING

Revelation 1:3

Reading the Bible gives an overall picture of God's Word. Many people find it helpful to use a daily reading program, which takes them systematically through the Bible.

STUDYING

Acts 17:11

Studying the Scriptures leads to personal discoveries of God's truths. Writing down these discoveries helps you organize and remember them.

MEMORIZING

Psalm 119:9,11

Memorizing God's Word enables use of the Sword of the Spirit to overcome Satan and temptations. You will have it readily available for witnessing or helping others with a "word in season."

MEDITATING

Psalm 1:2-3

Meditation is the thumb of "The Word Hand," for it is used in conjunction with each of the other methods. Only as you meditate on God's Word—thinking of its meaning and application in your life—will you discover its transforming power at work within you.

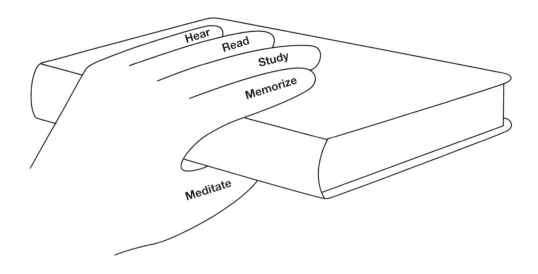

The Prayer Spoke
See John 15:7; Philippians 4:6-7

Prayer is a natural response to God as you hear him speak to you through his Word. It is sharing your heart with the One who longs for your companionship and who cares about your concerns. Prayer unleashes the power of God in your personal battles and in the lives of those for whom you pray.

Pray with your friends so that they see how you pray.

THE HORIZONTAL DIMENSION

How You Relate to Others
The Fellowship Spoke
See Matthew 18:20; Hebrews 10:24-25

Learning from and encouraging others creates chemistry that is pleasing to God. God has directed Christians to build each other up through interdependence and loving relationships with each other.

The Witnessing Spoke
See Matthew 4:19; Romans 1:16

The natural overflow of a rich, vibrant life in Christ should be sharing with others how they, too, can have this life. God has given believers the privilege and responsibility of reaching the world with the good news about Christ. You have been through this course, so you should be able to give your friends some pointers on how to share the gospel. If they are ready, perhaps you could lead them through this material yourself.

To be a disciple means to become like one's master. Discipleship is not an event but rather a lifelong process. The material given here is to provide you with a basic understanding of what to do once a person has come to faith. Eventually, it is important to get your friends into a vibrant community of believers so that they grow.

When people come to faith, it's important to help them grow in their newfound relationship with Jesus Christ. I know of no better tool to help them do this than the Navigators 2:7 series. *Growing Strong in God's Family*, the first book in the series, is designed to help you build a strong foundation for your Christian life through enriching Bible study, Scripture memory, and group interaction. With its biblical and practical approach to discipleship, this workbook will yield long-term, life-changing results.

KEEP GOING!

As you've worked through *Acts 29*, you've taken significant steps in becoming equipped to share your faith. You have:

- Learned about the process of evangelism (cultivating, sowing, harvesting, and multiplying)
- Taken significant Faith Steps in building relationships with those who don't follow Jesus as Lord

- Developed a prayer list—your Acts 29 Prayer Circle—and you've prayed for people who aren't yet following Jesus

Now, you might be asking, "Where do I go from here?" You can continue to grow and be fruitful in sharing your faith by:

- Continuing to meet as a group to share stories, keep each other accountable, encourage each other, and pray for each other and those you are sharing your faith with
- Forming a smaller group of two to four people who will meet as a group to share stories, keep each other accountable, encourage each other, and pray for each other and those you are sharing with
- Maintaining a consistent and meaningful quiet time with God
- Memorizing additional Scripture passages that deal with the importance of sharing your faith
- Keeping up on your Acts 29 Prayer Circle

Congratulations! You've finished *Acts 29*!

"Without a clear disciple-making purpose and strategy, various ministry programs — no matter how well intentioned the design — prove ineffective. Why? Because the programs keep people occupied but not developed enough to experience the rewards and responsibilities spiritual maturity brings. Furthermore, without substantive equipping, individuals can more easily slip from those programs back into the passive fringe of the Christian community. With good reason, Christ's command to 'make disciples' represents the purpose of ministry, not an afterthought. And discipleship doesn't happen by sitting in a spiritual greenhouse, but by design, effort, and perseverance on an individual level."

— Ron Bennett, *Intentional Disciplemaking*

APPENDIX A

THE BRIDGE TO LIFE[1]

Your non-Christian friends might have a lot of questions before they're ready to trust Christ. But at some point, you'll want to provide a clear explanation of the gospel and how each individual must respond to receive God's gift.

You can use "The Bridge" to present the gospel message clearly. You can sketch out this tool anytime, anywhere, in ten to fifteen minutes. When you share "The Bridge" with a friend, you walk him or her through four major points of the gospel message:

1. God's Love and His Plan
2. Humanity's Problem
3. God's Remedy: The Cross
4. Humanity's Response

These four steps lead to the fifth step: Receiving Christ as Savior.

As you draw out the illustration, turn to each Scripture reference and ask your friend to read it. Each step of "The Bridge" includes several questions you can ask to help you understand what your friend thinks about his or her relationship with God.

Once you've memorized "The Bridge," invite a Christian friend to lunch or coffee. Practice drawing the illustration on a table napkin, and ask your Christian friend to give you feedback.

Then invite a non-Christian friend out for lunch and share the gospel using this tool!

STEP 1: GOD'S LOVE AND HIS PLAN

Jesus said, "I have come that they may have life, and have it to the full" (John 10:10).

God created us in his own image to be his friend, to experience a full life assured of his love, and to bring him glory. But he didn't make us robots—he gave us freedom to choose to follow him.

Questions to ask your friend:
1. What do you think it means to live life to the fullest?
2. How are mankind and God different?
3. If God planned for us to experience peace and abundant life right now, why do most people not have this experience?

STEP 2: OUR PROBLEM: SEPARATION FROM GOD

"For all have sinned and fall short of the glory of God" (Romans 3:23).

When people choose to disobey God, the consequence is death. This death is both physical and spiritual (eternal spiritual separation from God in hell).

Questions to ask your friend:
1. What do you think is wrong with humanity?
2. When you think of death, what comes to mind?

STEP 3: GOD'S REMEDY: THE CROSS

"For Christ died for sins once for all, the righteous for the unrighteous, to bring you to God. He was put to death in the body but made alive by the Spirit" (1 Peter 3:18).

On our own, we can't attain the perfect and sinless life needed to bridge the gap between ourselves and God. Only Christ's death adequately pays for our sin and bridges the gulf between us and God. Christ died on the cross and rose from the grave, paying the penalty for our sin.

Questions to ask your friend:
1. If death can be defined as separation from God, how would you define life?
2. Why did Christ die?

STEP 4: HUMANITY'S RESPONSE

"I tell you the truth, whoever hears my words and believes him who sent me has eternal life and will not be condemned; he has crossed over from death to life" (John 5:24).

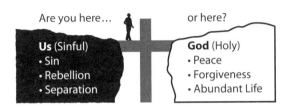

Believing means trust and commitment—acknowledging our sinfulness, trusting Christ's forgiveness, and letting him control our lives. Eternal life is a gift we each must receive.

Questions to ask your friend:
1. Where would you place yourself in this illustration?
2. Can you think of any reason you shouldn't cross over to God's side?

STEP 5: ASSURANCE OF SALVATION

"He who has the Son has life; he who does not have the Son of God does not have life. I write these things to you who believe in the name of the Son of God so that you may know that you have eternal life" (1 John 5:12-13).

How to receive Christ:
1. Admit your need (I am a sinner).
2. Be willing to turn from your sins (repent).
3. Believe that Jesus Christ died for you on the cross and rose from the grave.
4. Submit to Jesus' authority in your life.

OTHER TOOLS FOR SHARING THE GOSPEL

TOOL 1: THE STORY OF THE GOOD KING[1]

The following story provides a great illustration of how, through Christ, God came as a human to redeem and restore all of creation. In this wonderful story, you'll find the concepts of mankind's rebellion and depravity, God's love, the Incarnation, and salvation.

Once upon a time, a good and kind king ruled a great kingdom with many wonderful cities. However, in one distant city, people took advantage of the freedom the king gave them and started doing evil. They profited by their evil and began to fear that the king would interfere and throw them in jail. Eventually, these rebels seethed with hatred for the king. Convinced they would be better off without the king, the people declared their independence from the kingdom.

Soon, as the people did whatever they wanted, disorder reigned in the city and it became filled with violence, hatred, lying, oppression, murder, rape, slavery, and fear.

The king thought, *What should I do? If I send my army to conquer the city by force, the people will have to fight against me and I'll have to kill so many of them. And the rest will submit only through fear or intimidation, which will make them hate me even more. How would it help them to be dead or imprisoned or secretly seething with rage? But if I leave them alone, they'll destroy each other. And it breaks my heart to think of the pain they're causing and experiencing.*

So the king did something very surprising. He took off his robes and dressed in the rags of a homeless wanderer. Incognito, he entered the city and began living in a vacant lot near a garbage dump. He took up a trade—fixing broken pottery and furniture. Whenever people came to him, his kindness, goodness, fairness, and respect were so striking that they often lingered just to be in his presence. They revealed their fears to him, asked questions, and sought his advice.

He also gently told them that the rebels had fooled them and the true king had a better way to live, which he exemplified and taught. One by one, and eventually by the hundreds, people expressed confidence in him and began to live in his way.

Their influence spread to others, and the movement grew and grew. Eventually, the whole city regretted its rebellion and wanted to return to the kingdom again. Ashamed of their horrible mistake, they were afraid to approach the king, believing he would destroy them for their rebellion. Then the king-in-disguise told them the good news: He was himself the king and he loved them. He forgave them, held nothing against them, and welcomed them back into his kingdom. With his gentle and subtle presence, he accomplished what never could have been done through brute force.

TOOL 2: THE FOUR SPIRITUAL LAWS[2]

Just as physical laws govern the physical universe, spiritual laws govern our relationship with God. (When possible, read Scripture references from the Bible.)

Law 1: God *LOVES* you and offers a wonderful *PLAN* for your life.
God's Love
"God so loved the world that he gave his one and only Son, that whoever believes in him shall not perish but have eternal life" (John 3:16).

God's Plan
[Christ speaking] "I came that they may have life, and have it abundantly" [that it might be full and meaningful] (John 10:10, NASB).

Why do most people not experience a full and meaningful life? Because . . .

Law 2: People are *SINFUL* and *SEPARATED* from God. Therefore, they can't know and experience God's love and plan for life.
Man Is Sinful
"All have sinned and fall short of the glory of God" (Romans 3:23).

God created us to have fellowship with him. But because of our stubborn self-will, we choose to go our own independent way, preventing our fellowship with God. This self-will, characterized by an attitude of active rebellion or passive indifference, is evidence of what the Bible calls sin.

Man Is Separated
"The wages of sin is death" [spiritual separation from God] (Romans 6:23).

This diagram illustrates that God is holy and people are sinful. A great gulf separates us from God. The arrows illustrate that we continually try to reach God and the abundant life through our own efforts—such as a good life, philosophy, or religion—but inevitably we fail.

The third law explains the only way to bridge this gulf . . .

Law 3: Jesus Christ is God's *ONLY* provision for man's sin. Through him you can know and experience God's love and plan for your life.
Christ Died in Our Place
"God demonstrates His own love toward us, in that while we were yet sinners, Christ died for us" (Romans 5:8, NASB).

Christ Rose from the Dead
"Christ died for our sins. . . . He was buried. . . . He was raised on the third day according to the Scriptures. . . . He appeared to Peter, then to the Twelve. After that he appeared to more than five hundred" (1 Corinthians 15:3-6).

Christ Is the Only Way to God
"Jesus said to him, 'I am the way, and the truth, and the life; no one comes to the Father but through Me'" (John 14:6, NASB).

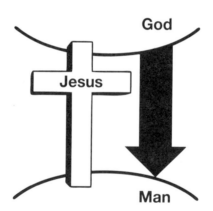

This diagram illustrates that God bridges the gulf that separates us from him by sending his Son, Jesus Christ, to die on the cross in our place in order to pay the penalty for our sins.

However, *it's not enough to only know these three laws . . .*

Law 4. We must individually *RECEIVE* Jesus Christ as Savior and Lord; then we can know and experience God's love and plan for our lives.
We Must Receive Christ
"As many as received Him, to them He gave the right to become children of God, even to those who believe in His name" (John 1:12, NASB).

We Receive Christ Through Faith
"By grace you have been saved through faith; and that not of yourselves, it is the gift of God; not as a result of works, so that no one may boast" (Ephesians 2:8-9, NASB).

When We Receive Christ, We Experience a New Birth

"Now there was a man of the Pharisees named Nicodemus, a member of the Jewish ruling council. He came to Jesus at night and said, 'Rabbi, we know you are a teacher who has come from God. For no one could perform the miraculous signs you are doing if God were not with him.'

"In reply Jesus declared, 'I tell you the truth, no one can see the kingdom of God unless he is born again.'

"'How can a man be born when he is old?' Nicodemus asked. 'Surely he cannot enter a second time into his mother's womb to be born!'

"Jesus answered, 'I tell you the truth, no one can enter the kingdom of God unless he is born of water and the Spirit. Flesh gives birth to flesh, but the Spirit gives birth to spirit. You should not be surprised at my saying, 'You must be born again.' The wind blows wherever it pleases. You hear its sound, but you cannot tell where it comes from or where it is going. So it is with everyone born of the Spirit'" (John 3:1-8).

We Receive Christ by Personal Invitation

[Christ speaking] "Behold, I stand at the door and knock; if anyone hears My voice and opens the door, I will come in to him" (Revelation 3:20, NASB).

Receiving Christ involves turning to God from self (repentance) and trusting Christ to come into our lives to forgive our sins and make us what he wants us to be. Just agreeing intellectually that Jesus Christ is the Son of God and that he died on the cross for our sins isn't enough. It's not enough to have an emotional experience. We receive Jesus Christ by faith, as an act of the will.

These two circles represent two kinds of lives:

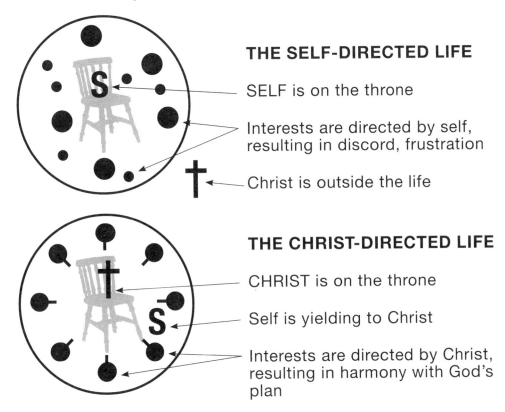

THE SELF-DIRECTED LIFE

SELF is on the throne

Interests are directed by self, resulting in discord, frustration

Christ is outside the life

THE CHRIST-DIRECTED LIFE

CHRIST is on the throne

Self is yielding to Christ

Interests are directed by Christ, resulting in harmony with God's plan

- Which circle best describes your life?

- Which circle would you like to have represent your life?

You can receive Christ right now by faith through prayer (prayer is simply talking to God). God knows your heart and isn't concerned with your words as much he is with the attitude of your heart. The following is a suggested prayer:

"Lord Jesus, I need you. Thank you for dying on the cross for my sins. I open the door of my life and receive you as my Savior and Lord. Thank you for forgiving my sins and giving me eternal life. Take control of the throne of my life. Make me the kind of person you want me to be."

TOOL 3: ZELEUCUS

The following story provides a great illustration of how, in Christ, God meets both the requirements of the law and the law of love. If you tell this story to others, ask how they'd respond if someone demonstrated such love to them. Would they continue to be a thief, or would they become a loyal son to their King and Father?

Long ago, a great king named Zeleucus became one of the first kings to write laws that governed his kingdom. His laws were fair and just and reflected his own love of virtue. Anyone who violated his laws faced the corresponding punishment.

One day, the king's magistrate brought before him a thief for sentencing. According to the Zeleucus' law, anyone caught stealing was to have both of his eyes gouged out. When the king looked up, he was heartbroken to see that the perpetrator was his own son!

The king thought, *What should I do? If I deal with my son justly, he'll lose both of his eyes. He'll never be able to enjoy another sunset or see his firstborn child. The thought of his losing his eyes breaks my heart. However, if I don't administer justice, then I will no longer be a just king.*

So the king did something very surprising. He took off his royal robe and had one of his own eyes gouged out and one of his son's eyes gouged out. By doing so, Zeleucus met the requirements of the law that two eyes be gouged out, and he also demonstrated love and compassion to the son he so loved.

THE ACTS 29 PRAYER CIRCLE

Use the following diagram to organize your prayers for people you love and want to see come into a vibrant relationship with Jesus Christ.

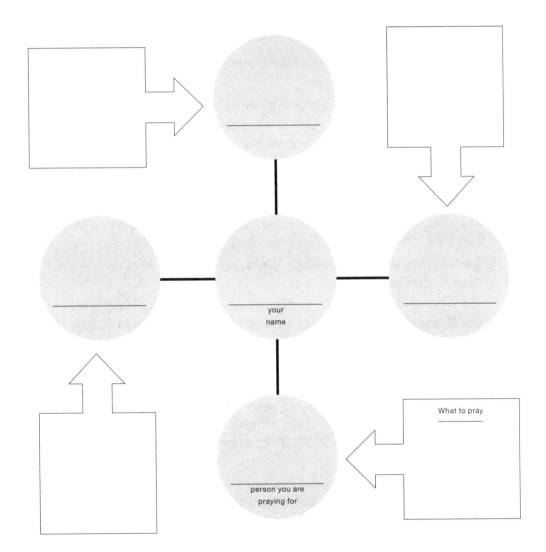

In the middle circle, write your own name. In the surrounding circles, write the names of four people you want to pray for. Each of the four circles has a corresponding box. In the box, write the specific prayer requests for each person. The next section offers some suggested prayers for non-Christians based upon biblical passages.

WHAT TO PRAY FOR SOMEONE
WHO DOESN'T YET KNOW CHRIST

The following list isn't an exhaustive list of what to pray for people you love who aren't following Jesus; rather, it provides some biblical ideas to get you started. Ideally, use this list while also asking God to lead and direct about both whom to pray for and what to pray.

Pray:
- That God would reveal himself to them (see Isaiah 65:1)
- That God would enable your friends to understand the gospel (see Matthew 13:19)
- That they would receive the Word of God and bear fruit (see Matthew 13:23)
- That God would reveal to them who Jesus Christ is (see Matthew 16:16-17)
- That God would confirm the gospel in their lives in a way that is meaningful to them (see Mark 16:20)
- That God would open their minds so they can understand the Scriptures (see Luke 24:45)
- That God would give them power to receive him and become one of his children (see John 1:12-13)
- That God would draw them to himself (see John 6:44)
- That God would convict them of their sin of unbelief in Jesus and that he would convict them of Jesus' resurrection and Jesus' victory over evil (see John 16:8-11)
- That God would open their hearts to responding to the gospel (see Acts 16:14)
- That God would create in them a hunger to seek him and reach out for him (see Acts 17:26-27)
- That God would cause the message that has been planted within them to grow (see 1 Corinthians 3:5-9)
- That God would remove whatever the Enemy is using to blind their minds and that God would help them see the light of the gospel of the glory of Christ (see 2 Corinthians 4:3-4)
- That God would enable you to verbally communicate the gospel to them (see Galatians 1:16)
- That God would make them alive in Christ (see Ephesians 2:4-5)
- That God would give them the faith to repent and be saved (see Ephesians 2:8-9)
- That God would rescue them from darkness and bring them into the kingdom of Christ (see Colossians 1:13-14)
- That God would cause the gospel to come to them with power, the Holy Spirit, and deep conviction (see 1 Thessalonians 1:5)
- That they would accept the Word of God as being from God (see 1 Thessalonians 2:13)
- That you would be able to gently instruct them (see 2 Timothy 2:25)
- That God would grant them repentance leading to a knowledge of the truth and that they would come to their senses and escape from the trap of the Devil, who has taken them captive to do his will (see 2 Timothy 2:26)

BOOKS TO READ AND TO LOAN

A vast wealth of Christian literature deals with the issues and questions most people face. If non-Christian friends don't seem ready to go directly to the Bible, try to find out what they're struggling with and offer a book dealing with that topic.

Of course, you should read the book yourself before loaning it out or giving it away. Thinking deeply about a broad range of topics will help you as you talk to friends about Christ. Ask if you can get together to discuss the book at a later date to keep your relationship and dialogue going.

The following books deal with some commonly asked questions.

QUESTIONS ABOUT PAIN AND SUFFERING

The Problem of Pain, by C. S. Lewis (San Francisco: HarperCollins, 1996). Lewis attempts to answer the question "If God is good and all-powerful, why does he allow his creatures to suffer pain?" This book provides a solid treatment of the question, and the author's writing style is geared toward those who have a philosophical bent.

Where Is God When It Hurts? by Philip Yancey (Grand Rapids, MI: Zondervan, 1990). Yancey explores the difficult issue of pain as it relates to God. Using biblical, personal, and current examples, he helps us understand why we suffer, how to cope, and how to reach out to someone in pain.

QUESTIONS ABOUT BIBLICAL AUTHORITY AND RELIABILITY

The Origin of the Bible, edited by Philip Wesley Comfort (Wheaton, IL: Tyndale, 1992). Comfort provides a comprehensive guide to the authority of the Bible, the origin of the Bible, the Bible text and manuscripts, and Bible translation.

The Case for Christ: A Journalist's Personal Investigation of the Evidence for Jesus, by Lee Strobel (Grand Rapids, MI: Zondervan, 1998). Strobel, the former legal editor of the *Chicago Tribune*, puts his journalism skills to work by interviewing a dozen experts with doctorates from some of the best universities in the world. The book deals with three main areas: Part 1 deals with the reliability of the biblical record, part 2 deals with the identity of Jesus, and part 3 deals with the resurrection of Jesus.

QUESTIONS ABOUT EVOLUTION AND CREATION

Refuting Evolution: A Handbook for Students, Parents, and Teachers Countering the Latest Arguments for Evolution, by Jonathan Sarfati (Green Forest, AR: Master Books, 1999). Sarfati, who holds a doctorate in physical chemistry and was the chess champion of Australia, wrote *Refuting Evolution* to counter a book written by the National Academy of Sciences, titled *Teaching About Evolution and the Nature of Science*. Sarfati deals with complex issues using language that people without science backgrounds can understand.

The Case for a Creator: A Journalist Investigates Scientific Evidence That Points Toward God, by Lee Strobel (Grand

Rapids, MI: Zondervan, 2004). In this book, Strobel presents discoveries from cosmology, biology, DNA research, astronomy, and physics that point to a Creator.

DEFENDING THE CHRISTIAN FAITH

Simply Christian: Why Christianity Makes Sense, by N. T. Wright (New York: HarperCollins, 2006). Wright presents a thoughtful look at the Christian faith by dealing with questions such as: Why do we expect justice? Why do we crave spirituality? Why are we attracted to beauty? Why are relationships so painful? How will the world be made right?

Mere Christianity, by C. S. Lewis (San Francisco: HarperCollins, 1952). In one of the most popular and beloved introductions to the Christian faith ever written, Lewis provides a powerful and rational case for the Christian faith.

UNDERSTANDING THE BIBLE

A Walk Through the Bible, by Lesslie Newbigin (Louisville, KY: Westminster, 1999). Newbigin takes the reader on a journey from Genesis through Revelation, concisely telling the story of the Bible in a way everyone can understand.

The Drama of Scripture: Finding Our Place in the Biblical Story, by Craig G. Bartholomew and Michael W. Goheen (Grand Rapids, MI: Baker, 2004). The authors take the reader through the entire Bible in a way that allows even those completely unfamiliar with Scripture to grasp the Bible as one unified story.

FIVE HOURS WITH JOHN[1]

In John 1, we read that after encountering Jesus, Andrew found his brother Peter and brought him to Jesus. Today, the equivalent of bringing individuals to Jesus is getting them into the Word of God. As they interact with the living Word of God, they'll meet Jesus.

The following material will help you get started on the exciting journey of introducing people to Jesus Christ. As you guide friends through these five studies of John, you'll want to keep these thoughts in mind:

- Your role is to love other people and help them make sense of the Bible. Leave the rest to the Holy Spirit and the Word of God.
- Because the primary issue for many non-Christians is the matter of Jesus' identity, that's the focus of these studies of John. We can summarize the scope of this emphasis with just two questions: (1) Who is Jesus? and (2) What does Jesus want of me?
- Don't feel the need to rigidly follow the questions provided here. Discussions will never go quite the way you think they will. The objective isn't to cover all the material; it's simply to help the other person understand what the Bible says.
- Maintain a sense of progress. Try to get through a chapter at each meeting.
- Instead of holding this book at each Bible study meeting, try one of these options: (1) writing the questions in the margin of your Bible, (2) producing enough copies of the questions for everyone in the group (just provide the questions, not the "Notes"), or (3) doing your best to know the material without the aid of a sheet of paper.
- Throughout these studies of John, you will find "Notes." These will help you understand the passages, deal with questions raised by your study, and simply help you if your group gets stuck. You don't need to make sure your group learns everything in the Notes. Be selective in what you explain so people don't feel as though they're ignorant or you're preaching.
- If an individual comes to faith before you finish all five studies, just continue to the next study.

The whole Christian life can be summarized in the two questions we noted earlier: (1) Who is Jesus? and (2) What does he want of me?

If group members come to faith in the midst of these studies, rejoice with them over their spiritual birth. Then proceed, paying special attention to the second question: "What does he want of me?" The gospel of John contains some of the greatest follow-up material ever written.

Remember that at the beginning, most people are committed to you for just one study at a time. Even in later stages, only you will be aware of the extensiveness of the process.

STUDY 1: JOHN 1:1-14

Read John 1:1-14

1. What did John mean when he spoke of "the Word" in verses 1-3 and 14?

2. Why do you think he is described as the Word?

Note: The function of a word is to transmit an idea. If I say "pencil," you immediately know what I mean. When I say "God," what comes to your mind? Where does your concept of God come from? Jesus Christ is the "Word" for God (see John 1:18).

3. What qualities do you see attributed to the Word in verses 1-5 and 14?

4. In verses 4-9, John used the word *light* as another analogy to describe Christ. What, to you, does this analogy imply (see also 3:19-21; 8:12; 12:35-36)?

5. John 1:9 says that every person is illuminated by Christ. In what sense do you think John meant this?

Note: God created all people, and all have life from him. But mankind abandoned this source of life and fell into darkness. While we still have traces of this noble origin, they're merely the remains of what we once were. What do you think does remain? Perhaps it's a certain God-consciousness? We all have a certain knowledge of God in a way similar to knowing something about an artist by viewing his works (see Romans 2:14-15).

These two elements explain the existence of religions and philosophies—a "God" notion and a standard of morality of which this God is the guardian. However, only by returning to the Light can we be illuminated and therefore reoriented. Life is in him. We understand life—our own and others'—by coming to the Light.

6. According to John 1:11-13, how do we enter God's family?

Note: It doesn't happen through:
- Heredity
- Self-effort
- The efforts of another (pastor, priest, and so on)

Only God can give life.

7. What do you think it means to "receive Christ"?

Note: In John 1:12, *receive* and *believe* are synonymous. In 3:36, the opposite of believing is rebelling against God—not accepting his authority over our lives. What do you conclude from this? *Believe* implies submission (see Revelation 3:20).

STUDY 2: JOHN 1:15-51

Read John 1:15-28

1. What claims did John the Baptist and John the writer make about Christ in verses 15-18?

Note: The writer of this gospel never named himself. In John 1 and elsewhere, "John" refers to John the Baptist, a well-known, radical prophet of Jesus' day.

2. What do you know about the Law that Moses gave (see 1:17)? Why do you think it was given?

Note: The Law wasn't given to be kept but to reveal sin for what it was. Like an X-ray, the Law doesn't cure anything; it simply reveals the problem (see John 5:45; Romans 3:19-20; 7:7; Galatians 2:16; 3:24).

3. Based on John 1:23, how do you understand the primary role of John the Baptist (see also John 3:26-30; Luke 3:4-14; 7:29-30)?

Note: John the Baptist announced the imminent arrival of the Messiah, calling people to make their way straight—a way that had been twisted by centuries of self-will and religious traditions. If they didn't do this, they wouldn't recognize the Messiah.

4. How could the people of Israel straighten their way of living?

Note: Repentance means a change in mentality—a desire to leave one's current way of life in order to enter into a relationship with Christ. Notice that the change came first, then the baptism. John's baptism was the sign that the individual had indeed repented (see Luke 3:4-14).

Read John 1:29-34
5. Why do you think John called Jesus the "Lamb of God" (see Isaiah 53:4-7; Hebrews 10:1-14)?

Note: The Old Testament sacrifices are illustrations of the need for the single and sufficient sacrifice of Christ.

6. What do you think John the Baptist's declaration in John 1:33 that Jesus would baptize with the Holy Spirit means?

Note: Being a Christian doesn't merely mean following a certain philosophy or becoming a part of a religious system; rather, it's a relationship between two individuals: Jesus Christ and you (see 1:12; 3:5-8; 4:23-24). Also, note that this baptism doesn't involve water.

Read John 1:35-51
7. This section teaches the story of how five people first encountered Christ. Each one came by a different means. Who are the five, and what prompted each one to believe in Christ?

STUDY 3: JOHN 2

Read John 2:1-11
1. What do you think Jesus' attendance at the wedding indicates about him (see Matthew 11:16-19)?
2. Do you find Jesus' solution to the problem of no wine at the wedding believable? Why or why not?

Note: What claim does John 1:3 make about Jesus? It would be hard to imagine the Creator appearing on earth without revealing his power over his creation. Christ, fully understanding the nature of matter and having power over it, could command the elements of creation at will (see Hebrews 11:3).

3. Notice in John 2:11 that John described the event as a "miraculous sign." He consistently used this phrase to refer to Jesus' miracles (see 3:2; 4:54; 6:14,26). Why? What's the function of a sign?

Note: Signs serve to inform.

4. What does the sign tell us about Jesus?
5. How do you understand this conversation between Jesus and his mother (see 2:3-5)?

Note: Woman was an expression of endearment. What Jesus said could be paraphrased as follows: "We are not of the same world. What is a problem for you is nothing for me. I'll take care of it. I have time for such things before my 'hour' comes."

6. What time do you think Jesus referred to in John 2:4 (see also 7:6; 12:23,27; 17:1)?

Note: Jesus' death wasn't a futile and unforeseen tragedy; it was the reason he came to earth. The "miraculous signs" contributed to setting off the chain reaction that inevitably led to his death.

Read John 2:12-22

7. What do you think prompted Jesus to act the way he did when he cleared the temple (see verses 13-17)?

Note: Passover was one of the principal religious feasts of the Jews. They came to Jerusalem for celebration and spiritual cleansing. However, the temple merchants exploited the situation by selling animals and exchanging foreign currencies for the temple currency—all for profit. Jesus accused the merchants of soiling God's name. In essence, he told them, "Don't use my Father's name to promote your dirty business!" (see Romans 2:24).

8. How can Jesus' anger be justified (see Romans 1:18)?
9. The Jews demanded that Jesus show his credentials for such authoritative actions. What do you learn about Jesus from his answer (see John 2:18-22)?
10. Why do you think Jesus' resurrection would constitute the ultimate credential (see 1 Corinthians 15:12-19)?

Read John 2:23-25

11. Why do you think Jesus didn't respond to the people in 2:23 even though it says they believed in him?

Note: Real belief implies commitment. Their acceptance of Jesus didn't go that far (see John 12:42-43; James 2:19). A faith where the individual reserves the right to run his or her own life isn't faith at all (see John 3:36).

STUDY 4: JOHN 3

Read John 3:1-14

1. What stands out to you about Nicodemus's observations concerning Jesus (see verses 1-2)?
2. Jesus corrected Nicodemus in verse 3. According to Jesus, when is someone qualified to understand the things of God (see John 1:12-13; 1 Corinthians 2:7-16)?

Note: Jesus said that Nicodemus couldn't come to any meaningful conclusions about the things of God without being "born again."

3. What shows that Nicodemus didn't understand spiritual matters (see John 3:4,9)?

Note: God speaks on a spiritual level. As humans, we interpret him on human terms and find it difficult to conceive of anything beyond those terms. For example, imagine a world of blind people attempting to comprehend the color red. Their failure to comprehend it doesn't preclude its existence. To "see" the kingdom of God, we need to acquire spiritual senses.

4. How do you understand "born again" in 3:3-8?

Note: Being reborn implies that:

- A person was dead in some sense and is now alive in that area. The Holy Spirit makes a formerly dead spirit alive (see Ephesians 2:1-9).
- A person has a new parent. Believers are born of God (see John 1:12-13), so they now have their Father's spiritual "genes."

5. Why do you think Jesus insists that one must be born again before he or she can see God's kingdom (see John 3:3,5,8; Ephesians 2:1-9)?

Note: You must have an alive spirit with the Father's spiritual "genes"—his traits and some of his abilities—in order to have the spiritual senses for seeing his kingdom.

6. What do you suppose being "born of water" means (see John 3:5)?

Note: Jesus probably referred to the baptism of John here. (That was the only kind of "water" Nicodemus was acquainted with.) However, this doesn't imply that someone must be baptized to be saved. John's baptism was unique—a symbol of repentance already in effect (see Luke 3:7-14).

The water didn't bring about the change; the repentance did. Repentance is necessary if spiritual birth is to take place (see Isaiah 55:6-7; Luke 13:1-5). Jesus was saying to Nicodemus, "Do what John the Baptist has said. Do an about-face, leaving your old way of thinking; then permit the Holy Spirit to enter you, giving you a new life."

By itself, John's message of repentance wasn't complete. It wasn't sufficient for spiritual life without the additional part of being "born of the Spirit" (see Acts 19:1-7).

Read John 3:14-21
7. The word *believe* appears several times in verses 15-18. What's the relationship between believing and being born again?
8. For what purpose did God send Christ (see verses 16-21)?

Read John 3:22-36
9. How did John the Baptist describe himself and his work (see verses 27-30)? What qualities characterized him?

Note: John the Baptist serves as a model for the manner in which we should tell others about Christ. He didn't call attention to himself but described himself as "a voice" (1:19-23) or as the best man at the wedding (see 3:27-30).

10. According to John 3:31-36, what needs to take place for a person to come to the conclusion that this message about God is the truth?
11. What did you learn about your relationship with God from our discussion of this chapter?

STUDY 5: JOHN 4

Read John 4:1-18

1. What do you learn about Jesus from these verses?

Note: In the first century, it was rare for a rabbi to talk to a woman, let alone to a Samaritan woman.

2. What do you think Jesus meant by "living water" (4:10; see also Isaiah 44:3-4; John 7:37-39)?
3. What claims did Jesus make about the very special water?
4. How do you understand the "thirst" Jesus talked about?

Note: Innate human dissatisfaction is strong.

5. How had the Samaritan woman previously tried to quench her thirst?

Note: She had been drinking at the wrong fountain—the fountain of promiscuity (see John 4:17-18; Isaiah 55:1-2).

6. Why do you think the woman didn't understand what Jesus meant by Living Water?

Note: She was thinking in the natural or physical realm, while Jesus was speaking of the supernatural (see John 3:4; 6:26,34).

Read John 4:19-30

7. As soon as the Samaritan woman perceived that the conversation was heading toward religion, she tried to keep it from becoming personal by employing a very common tactic. What was it (see verses 19-20)?

Note: She tried to draw Jesus into a general discussion on religion but one that didn't focus on her.

8. How did Jesus handle her evasive tactic (see verses 21-24)?

Note: It's not some religious system, forms, or creed that makes the difference. God's new temple is the individual, and that's where the worship is to take place (see 1 Corinthians 6:19).

9. What do we learn about Jesus from his declaration in John 4:26?
10. What decision did the woman face?
11. What happened to her water pot?

Read John 4:31-42

12. Why was Jesus no longer hungry (see verses 31-34)?

13. What is the harvest (see verse 35; Matthew 9:36-38)?

14. What conclusion did the people come to about Jesus? What was the basis of their thinking (see John 4:39-42)?

Read John 4:43-54

15. How do you interpret Jesus' reaction to the royal official's request? Compare the official's attitude with that of the official in Matthew 8:8.

16. Why do you think Jesus answered the request in spite of the man's imperfect faith?

NOTES

Introduction

1. Craig G. Bartholomew and Michael W. Goheen, *The Drama of Scripture: Finding Our Place in the Biblical Story* (Grand Rapids, MI: Baker, 2004), 7.
2. Used by permission of The Navigators, copyright 1999. All rights reserved. *The 2:7 Series, Course 1: The Growing Disciple* (Colorado Springs, CO: NavPress, 1979).

SESSION 1: Why Bother Sharing the Gospel?

1. Gordon J. Wenham, *Story as Torah: Reading the Old Testament Ethically* (Edinburgh, Scotland: T&T Clark, 2000), 37.
2. John I. Durham, *Exodus,* Word Biblical Commentary, Volume 3 (Waco, TX: Word, 1987), 263.
3. Charles Ryrie, *The Ryrie Study Bible* (Chicago: Moody, 1994), 93.
4. R. T. France, *Tyndale New Testament Commentaries: Matthew* (Grand Rapids, MI: Eerdmans, 1985), 319–320.
5. France, 320.
6. Craig Bartholomew and Michael W. Goheen, *The Drama of Scripture: Finding Our Place in the Biblical Story* (Grand Rapids, MI: Baker, 2004), 169.
7. F. F. Bruce, *The New International Commentary on the New Testament* (Grand Rapids, MI: Eerdmans, 1988), 36.
8. Larry Hurtado, *New International Biblical Commentary—Mark* (Peabody, MA: Hendrickson Publishers, 1989), 169.
9. W. E. Vine, *Vine's Expository Dictionary of Old and New Testament Words* (Nashville: Thomas Nelson, 1997), 612–613.

SESSION 2: The Process of Evangelism

1. William L. Lane, *The New International Commentary on the New Testament: The Gospel of Mark* (Grand Rapids, MI: Eerdmans, 1974), 149.
2. Lane, 153.
3. Larry Hurtado, *New International Biblical Commentary—Mark* (Peabody, MA: Hendrickson Publishers, 1989), 154.
4. Hurtado, 169.
5. John Calvin, *Commentary on the Epistles of Paul the Apostle to the Corinthians, Vol. 1* (Grand Rapids, MI: Baker, 1999), 127.
6. Adapted from the chart in K. C. Hinckley, *Living Proof: A Small Group Discussion Guide* (Colorado Springs, CO: NavPress, 1992).

SESSION 3: Understanding People and Their Culture

1. "The Jerry Springer Show," Wikipedia, http://en.wikipedia.org/wiki/The_Jerry_Springer_Show.

2. Jim Petersen, *Living Proof: Sharing the Gospel Naturally* (Colorado Springs, CO: NavPress, 1989), 29–30.

3. Gerhard Von Rad, *Genesis: A Commentary*, trans. John H. Marks (Philadelphia: Westminster, 1961), 58.

4. Craig G. Bartholomew and Michael W. Goheen, *The Drama of Scripture: Finding Our Place in the Biblical Story* (Grand Rapids, MI: Baker, 2004), 35.

5. Gordon J. Wenham, *Word Biblical Commentary: Genesis 1–15* (Nashville: Thomas Nelson, 1987), 33.

6. W. E. Vine, *Vine's Expository Dictionary of New and Old Testament Words* (Nashville: Thomas Nelson, 1997), 268.

7. John Calvin, *Calvin's Commentaries on the Book of Genesis* (Grand Rapids, MI: Baker, 1999), 151.

8. Bartholomew and Goheen, 44.

9. R. E. Allen, ed., *The Oxford Dictionary of Current English* (Oxford, England: Oxford University Press, 1984), 177.

10. Richard Middleton and Brian J. Walsh, *The Transforming Vision: Shaping a Christian World View* (Downers Grove, IL: InterVarsity, 1984), 32.

11. F. F. Bruce, *The New International Commentary on the New Testament: The Book of Acts* (Grand Rapids, MI: Eerdmans, 1988), 329.

12. Kenneth L. Barker, ed., *The NIV Study Bible* (Grand Rapids, MI: Zondervan, 1984), 2284.

13. Barker, 2285; and Marshall, *The NIV Study Bible* (Grand Rapids, MI: Zondervan, 1984), 289.

SESSION 4: Taking Stock of Your Spiritual Resources

1. J. I. Packer, *Keep in Step with the Spirit* (Grand Rapids, MI: Baker, 1984), 65–66.

2. Lesslie Newbigin, quoted in Leon Morris, *The New International Commentary on the New Testament: The Gospel According to John* (Grand Rapids, MI: Eerdmans, 1995), 619.

3. W. E. Vine, *Vine's Expository Dictionary of Old and New Testament Words* (Nashville: Thomas Nelson), 200.

4. Vine, 737–738.

5. Charles Spurgeon, *12 Sermons on the Holy Spirit* (Grand Rapids, MI: Baker, 1973), 122.

6. The Navigators, *Growing Strong in God's Family: A Course in Personal Discipleship to Strengthen Your Walk with God* (Colorado Springs, CO: NavPress: 1999), 52.

7. John Stott, *Between Two Worlds: The Challenge of Preaching Today* (Grand Rapids, MI: Eerdmans, 1982), 97.

8. The Navigators, 66.

9. R. T. France, *Tyndale New Testament Commentaries: Matthew* (Grand Rapids, MI: Eerdmans, 1985), 175.

10. France, 175.

11. Joel B. Green, *The New International Commentary of the New Testament: The Gospel of Luke* (Grand Rapids, MI: Eerdmans, 1997), 413.

12. Vine, 1160.

13. C. E. B. Cranfield, *Romans: A Shorter Commentary* (Grand Rapids, MI: Eerdmans, 1985), 303.

14. Douglas J. Moo, *The New International Commentary on the New Testament: The Epistle to the Romans* (Grand Rapids, MI: Eerdmans, 1996), 788–799.

SESSION 5: Making Christ Known in Your World

1. The ideas and thoughts in this section come from Mike Shamy, *Six Critical Factors Studies*: Critical Factor 2 (Unpublished, 2002), 7–18.

2. W. E. Vine, *Vine's Expository Dictionary of Old and New Testament Words* (Nashville: Thomas Nelson, 1997), 55.

3. Thomas A. Wolf, *Oikos Evangelism: The Biblical Pattern*, http://www.kristenonline.com/download/book/

oikos%20evangelism.pdf.

4. Leon Morris, *The New International Commentary of the New Testament: The Gospel According to John* (Grand Rapids, MI: Eerdmans, 1995), 140.

5. Rodney Stark, *The Rise of Christianity: How the Obscure, Marginal Jesus Movement Became the Dominant Religious Force in the Western World in a Few Centuries* (Princeton, NJ: HarperCollins, 1996), 208.

6. Michael Green, *Evangelism in the Early Church* (Grand Rapids, MI: Eerdmans, 1970), 207.

7. F. F. Bruce, *The New International Commentary on the New Testament: The Book of Acts* (Grand Rapids, MI: Eerdmans, 1988), 201.

8. Merrill C. Tenney, *The Zondervan Pictorial Encyclopedia of the Bible* (Grand Rapids, MI: Zondervan, 1976), 680.

9. Shamy, 29.

10. J. Oswald Sanders, *Spiritual Leadership* (Chicago: Moody, 1994), 95.

SESSION 6: Living Out the Gospel

1. Merrill C. Tenney, *The Zondervan Pictorial Encyclopedia of the Bible* (Grand Rapids, MI: Zondervan, 1976), 220.

2. Charles Ryrie, ed., *The Ryrie Study Bible* (Chicago: Moody, 1994), 155.

3. Tenney, 933.

4. R. T. France, *Tyndale New Testament Commentaries: Matthew* (Grand Rapids, MI: Eerdmans, 1985), 112.

5. Gordon D. Fee, *The New International Commentary on the New Testament: Paul's Letter to the Philippians* (Grand Rapids, MI: Eerdmans, 1995), 247.

6. *The Analytical Greek Lexicon* (Grand Rapids, MI: Zondervan, 1976), 366.

7. F. F. Bruce, *The New International Commentary on the New Testament: The Epistle to the Colossians, to Philemon, and to the Ephesians* (Grand Rapids, MI: Eerdmans, 1984), 174.

8. Bruce, 175.

9. Leon Morris, *The New International Commentary on the New Testament: The First and Second Epistles to the Thessalonians* (Grand Rapids, MI: Eerdmans, 1991), 131.

10. Peter H. Davids, *The New International Commentary on the New Testament: The First Epistle of Peter* (Grand Rapids, MI: Eerdmans, 1990), 116.

11. Davids, 116.

12. Philip H. Towner, *The New International Commentary on the New Testament: The Letters to Timothy and Titus* (Grand Rapids, MI: Eerdmans, 2006), 701.

13. W. E. Vine, *Vine's Expository Dictionary of Old and New Testament Words* (Nashville: Thomas Nelson, 1997), 1068.

14. Vine, 1057.

15. Vine, 1099.

16. Davids, 95.

SESSION 7: Embodying the Gospel Through Community

1. W. E. Vine, *Vine's Expository Dictionary of Old and New Testament Words* (Nashville: Thomas Nelson, 1997), 420.

2. Douglas J. Moo, *The New International Commentary on the New Testament: The Epistle to the Romans* (Grand Rapids, MI: Eerdmans, 1996), 777.

3. Vine, 461.

4. C. E. B. Cranfield, *The First Epistle of Peter* (London: SCM Press Ltd., 1950), 94–95.

5. Mike Shamy, *Six Critical Factors Studies* (Unpublished, 2002), 44.

6. Philip H. Towner, *The New International Commentary on the New Testament: The Letters to Timothy and Titus* (Grand Rapids, MI: Eerdmans, 2006), 739.

SESSION 8: Explaining the Gospel Through Words

1. W. E. Vine, *Vine's Expository Dictionary of Old and New Testament Words* (Nashville: Thomas Nelson, 1997), 873.

2. *The Analytical Greek Lexicon* (Grand Rapids, MI: Zondervan, 1976), 172.

3. Much of the material in these two paragraphs comes from Will Metzger, *Tell the Truth: The Whole Gospel to the Whole Person by the Whole Person* (Downers Grove, IL: InterVarsity, 1984), 42–43. In turn, Metzger credits Michael Green, *Evangelism in the Early Church* (Grand Rapids, MI: Eerdmans, 1970), 69–70.

4. F. F. Bruce, *The New International Commentary on the New Testament: The Book of the Acts* (Grand Rapids, MI: Eerdmans, 1988), 201.

5. Bruce, 212–213.

6. Bruce, 276.

7. Vine, 873.

8. Vine, 873.

9. Vine, 1132.

10. Vine, 924.

11. Vine, 1123.

12. J. I. Packer, *Evangelism and the Sovereignty of God* (Downers Grove, IL: InterVarsity, 1961), 47–48.

13. Vine, 565.

14. Michael Green, *Evangelism in the Early Church* (Grand Rapids, MI: Eerdmans, 1970), 229. In this book, Green convincingly showed that one of the main purposes of the gospel accounts was for evangelism.

15. Green, 223.

SESSION 9: Preparing Your Personal Testimony

1. *Shadowlands*, directed by Richard Attenborough (Ventura, CA: Price Entertainment, 1993).

2. Adapted from The Navigators, *Deepening Your Roots in God's Family: A Course in Personal Discipleship to Strengthen Your Walk with God — Book 2* (Colorado Springs, CO: NavPress, 1999), 57–63.

SESSION 10: Bringing in the Harvest

1. Wayne Grudem, *Systematic Theology: An Introduction to Biblical Doctrine* (Grand Rapids, MI: Zondervan, 1994), 699.

2. Grudem, 709.

3. W. E. Vine, *Vine's Expository Dictionary of Old and New Testament Words* (Nashville: Thomas Nelson, 1997), 401–402.

4. Augustus Hopkins Strong, *Systematic Theology* (Philadelphia: The Judson Press, 1912), 832.

5. Strong, 832.

6. Strong, 839.

7. Larry Hurtado, *New International Biblical Commentary — Mark* (Peabody, MA: Hendrickson Publishers, 1989), 72.

8. William L. Lane, *The New International Commentary on the New Testament: The Gospel of Mark* (Grand Rapids, MI: Eerdmans, 1974), 169–170.

9. Lane, 169.
10. Grudem, 715.
11. Vine, 108.
12. Grudem, 711.

SESSION 11: Discipling a New Believer

1. W. E. Vine, *Vine's Expository Dictionary of Old and New Testament Words* (Nashville: Thomas Nelson, 1997), 308.
2. "The Wheel Illustration," used by permission of The Navigators, copyright 1976, all rights reserved; http://www.navigators.org/us/resources/illustrations/items/The%20Wheel%20-%20Illustration.
3. "The Word Hand," used by permission of The Navigators, all rights reserved; http://www.navigators.org/us/resources/illustrations/items/The%20Word%20Hand.

APPENDIX A: The Bridge to Life

1. Reprinted (adapted) from "The Bridge Illustration," copyright 1969 by The Navigators. Used by permission of NavPress, http://www.navpress.com. All rights reserved. *The Bridge* is a booklet from NavPress.

APPENDIX B: Other Tools for Sharing the Gospel

1. Adapted from Brian McLaren, *A Generous Orthodoxy* (Grand Rapids, MI: Zondervan, 2004), 57–58. This story was originally written by St. Athanasius the Great, who lived in the fourth century. Athanasius was a theologian, pope of Alexandria, and a church father.
2. Used by permission of Bright Media Foundation and Campus Crusade for Christ.

APPENDIX E: Five Hours with John

1. Adapted from Jim Petersen, *Living Proof: Sharing the Gospel Naturally* (Colorado Springs, CO: NavPress, 1989), 217–226. The study was originally titled *24 Hours with John,* and it covered the entire gospel of John in twenty-four studies.

AUTHOR

CHRIS KOVAC completed his undergraduate degree in English at Acadia University, followed by a history degree at McMaster University and a master of divinity at McMaster Divinity College. He taught high school for four years, and since 2003 he has been working with The Navigators of Canada, directing a collegiate ministry at McMaster University.

Chris came to know Jesus personally while a student at Acadia University in Wolfville, Nova Scotia. He was individually and personally discipled by a Navigator who mentored him through an intentional process of spiritual growth. As a result, Chris has given himself to life-on-life discipleship, following Jesus as his model. He is passionate about God, his family, his ministry with The Navigators, sports, and music.

Chris and his wife, Darci, with their three children — Benjamin, Mikaela, and Moriah — live in Hamilton, Ontario.

Share your faith with more people. Let NavPress help you!

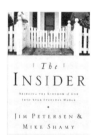